Z P C A S

A NEW DEAL FOR
SOUTH ATLANTIC

ALTAIR MAIA

ZPCAS - A new deal for South Atlantic
Author: Altair de Sousa Maia

Copyright @ by Altair Maia

ISBN: 9781670649423

1. Political Science
2. Foreign Trade
3. South America
4. Africa
5. Commercial Navigation in South Atlantic

I. Title.
ZPCAS - A New Deal for South Atlantic

ZPCAS Agreement: 25 countries. Three in South America and 22 in Africa.

Summary

Annex

Annex I – Lloyds – The biggest navigation company in South Hemisphere

Annex II – The Thailand Channel

Annex III - The movement of containers

Annex IV – The economic blocks in Africa and in South America

Annex V – The biggest vessel of the XVII century

The author

Other books

References

Notice:

*Any trade policy between South America and Africa will be doomed to failure if the issue of maritime transport is **not** addressed.*

Thanks to Nelson Bessa, an expert in Chinese affairs, for the support and revision of the text and concepts issued here.

Navigare necesse est; vivere non est necesse
(To navigate is necessary. To live is not)
Gen. Pompeo[1]

---

[1] *Gnaeus Pompey Magnum, a Roman general and politician (106-48 BC).*

For a long time the oceans represented the isolation of men on Earth. Today they do represent the link and the path of union among the nations of the different continents.

Preface

Scientists say that South America and Africa, which once were physically united in a supercontinent called Pangaea, have been slowly separating since the beginning of time.

However, there is another separation in progress, much faster, remarkable and disastrous than the physical separation of the continents. It is a commercial separation that has been imposed on us since the North hemisphere became connected across Suez and Panama channels.

South America and Africa trade interchange was intense in the past although based on the shameful slave trade. However, this deplorable kind of trade shaped somehow the relationship among our peoples all over the rest of the world and throughout History.

A few centuries ago, and for a long time, Brazil and West Africa formed an integrated economic region. Everything that was done in a side of the Atlantic Ocean spilled over on the other side. The South Atlantic - gathering Brazil and Africa – constituted, so to speak, an integrated economic system.

Our ties are indelible. Brazil is the largest black nation outside of Africa. We, Brazilians and Africans, are eager to resume those bonds that unite us and that have been falling apart over time.

There are no habits, ties, customs or traditions, that have sustained themselves without a commercial basis. The trade, the exchange of goods and services is, indeed, the "real link" that interlinks all other ties among different peoples.

Therefore, why do we separate ourselves commercially, if we have products that interest both sides to establish the principles of trade?

We could not say it is a case of lack of political will, because there is.

We could not say it is a case of lack of commercial interest because our economies are complementary: Africa produces numerous products of interest to the South American economies and so do South American economies with regards to West Africa.

What would be missing then for this trade to happen in large scale?

The answer is simple and straightforward: **lack of transport!**

Transport is the basis of all commercial exchanges and there is no significant direct transport lines between South America and Africa.

The cost of transportation between South America to Africa is double what it costs from Europe, the United States, China or Japan to Africa.

A good, fast and inexpensive maritime shipping system could increase the business in South Atlantic on an equal basis with the United States, Europe, India, China and Japan.

Equality of conditions in the competition for markets is sufficient for South America and Africa to emerge as major trading partners since the other ties mentioned above are still alive, and dormant waiting for an opportunity to manifest.

We are sure that an efficient transportation system in South Atlantic can be extremely profitable for both sides, substantially increasing our trade relations and bringing, in its wake, the rescue of all the other relations we have celebrated so much.

Chapter I

Considerations on navigation, transport and foreign trade

In the last five or six centuries, when the Europeans began long ocean journeys, "beyond the horizon", the Portuguese and Spanish ships, though still very rudimentary, represented a great technological leap at the time due to the recent discoveries or inventions that revolutionized the *modus navigare* in Europe.

Until the thirteenth century, Europeans, except for the Vikings, still did not know the secrets and mysteries of the open sea, of the winds and of the stars. Navigation was almost restricted to the inland seas around Europe: the Mediterranean Sea, as well as the Red Sea and coastal navigation in the North Atlantic in its European part. Only at the end of that century, Europeans would venture along the African coast and to the Canary Islands.

The ships used by the Portuguese, Spanish, English, French and others developed speeds of up to twelve knots[2]. Some others, like the ships of a class called "clipper", developed the "fantastic" speed of seventeen knots. To get an idea of what this means, current merchant ships develop speeds between twenty and twenty-five knots.

The shortest distance between Europe and South America is the distance between Portugal and the Brazilian Northeast, in the city of Touros in Rio Grande do Norte state, which is just over 5,600 kilometers from Lisbon.

This same region of the Rio Grande do Norte is a mere 2,500 kilometers away from the Island of Brava in the Archipelago of Cape Verde, being, therefore, the closest Brazilian region of Africa.

It is possible to imagine then that these ships would only need twelve days to leave Portugal, to cross the Atlantic and to arrive on the Brazilian coast. Great mistake: sailing navigation has its mysteries,

---

[2] *The "knot" is equal to one nautical mile, which is equal to 1.85 kilometers.*

because the winds do not always, or almost never, blow in the desired direction. Moreover, as said the philosopher Seneca[3]; there is no good wind for those who do not know where they want to go.

Knowing where to go was not enough. It was necessary to master the elements of nature that would permit us to arrive there.

In this specific case, even knowing where you want to go, the opposite wind turns the navigation much more difficult and complex, requiring the navigator much mastery and knowledge of the "soul" of the winds.

To navigate at the counter wind, it is necessary to make the navigation on the zigzag way, which triples or quadruples the distance and, therefore, the time to reach the other point.

The learning of navigation against the wind was what allowed reaching the desired point, even with the opposite wind. It was necessary to know "the hearth" of the winds.

Even though they were small, rustic and wind-propelled vessels, there was the flourishing of navigation and international trade in the South Atlantic in the sixteenth to nineteenth centuries. Trade and shipping between Brazil and the West Coast of Africa were intense.

Although the commercial exploitation of the Atlantic Ocean (South and North) started with the

---

[3] *Lucius Annaeus Seneca was born four years BC and died in the year 65. He was a great thinker of the Roman Empire*

voyages of Christopher Columbus, Vasco da Gama, Pedro Álvares Cabral and other brave sailors, not least important were the creation of three commercial shipping companies in the United Kingdom and the Netherlands.

The creation of these companies changed the *modus operandi* of the metropolis in Europe with the new colonies overseas. Before it was only domination and exploitation. Now the leitmotif was domination, exploitation and profit.

In Britain, the **Company of Merchants of London** was established in 1600. whose focus was the trading to the East Indies. In Holland, two other companies were established, the **VOC** and the **WIC**, to deal in the East Indies and the West Indies[4].

The Netherlands, following the model initiated between Portugal and Spain, divided the world between these two companies, granting each one of them the "monopoly" of the trade in their areas of operation.

The VOC Company, focused on its commercial exploitation of Asia's trade routes with the lucrative tea trade, which was also the commercial objective of the English company. The WIC was exploiting the trade routes of the Caribbean and the Americas, with the rich market of minerals, sugar and Africa´s trade routes with the slave deal.

Those three companies, unlike the exploitation practiced by the Spaniards and the Portuguese, were

---

[4] *VOC and WIC were two separate companies: the Vereenigde Oost-Indische Compagnie - VOC, established in 1602, and the West-Indische Compagnie - WIC, established in 1621.*

private-owned companies of capitalist character. While the Portuguese and Spanish colonies were wholly dependent on their metropolis, the Dutch and English colonies depended on their own profits[5].

European ships (Portuguese and Spaniards), which demanded the South Seas, came in search of gold, silver, precious stones, sugar, wood etc., and left in the Brazilian ports the goods needed to supply this market, which emerged strong and thriving south of the Equator.

Brazilian merchants used some of these goods as payment for the slaves they bought on the African coast (they bought of the Portuguese themselves in Africa who were the primary operators of the profitable slave trade).

A big quantity of these slaves was transported on ships of English or Dutch flag at the beginning of this shameful deal. Thus, by transporting goods and bringing slaves, the navigation and the deplorable slave trade between Africa and the Americas became ever more intense.

Brazil and Africa constituted, as it were, an "integrated economic system". African needs of manufactured goods were attended by Portuguese merchants from Brazil who, in turn, had their needs for slave labor supplied by the own Portuguese traders.

---

[5] *The history of Brazil is closely linked to these companies. Maurice of Nassau, the governor of Dutch Brazil (from 1637 to 1644), was hired by WIC company to make the Brazilian colony a profitable colony, with the sugar trade.*

With the end of slavery in the nineteenth century and the consequent collapse in the "importation" of slaves, navigation between Brazil and Africa began to fade. There was no longer the "commodity" of return.

The advent of steam-powered vessels in the end of the XVIII century and later the diesel-powered vessels, with greater autonomy of navigation without the need for refueling, was the "lime shovel" in maritime transport in the South Atlantic. Ships leaving Europe for Brazil or from Brazil to Europe no longer needed a "technical stop" in Africa.

Therefore, with no return "merchandise" and with the emergence of modern long-range ships without the need for stopovers, commercial shipping between these two continental "blocks" has become almost non-existent, being limited to bulk carriers scaling ports point to point.

Today, Brazil's and South America trade with Africa is concentrated in commodities. Over 70% of what we export to Africa is in this category and more than 90% of what we import from Africa as well.

Chapter II

The multilateral trade of the African continent

*Prior to the period of Europe's "big sailing", trade among the
African empires flowed strongly and freely.*

Navigation in the South Atlantic depends exclusively on foreign trade of Brazil, Argentina, and Uruguay, in South America side, and the countries of the West Coast of Africa, generating two significant but isolated commercial navigation flows without connection between them, each one seeking "the ways of the North".

Just over 150 years ago, this reality was completely different. All navigation from Europe or from the United States to Asia and/or to the West coast of the USA had passage through South Atlantic, reaching the Good Hope Cape at the tip of the African continent or the Strait of Magalhães at the tip of South America. However, this is now the past. The Suez and Panama Channels changed that history. Today the two continental blocks face several difficulties to keep the navigation service working.

According to the World Trade Organization (WTO) data. As can be seen in the table below. The African continent's trade flows (imports plus exports) with the world, is around one trillion dollars, reaching actually US$ 1.051.9 (one trillion and fifty one billion dollars) by the end of 2018, with a slightly unfavorable trade balance for Africans, with more imports than exports.

Africa: interchange of goods and services

US$ billion	World(1)	África	% world
Trade of goods - 2018			
Exports	19.475.0	478.0	2. 45
Imports	19.866.0	573.9	2. 88
Total chain goods	39.341.0	1,051.9	2. 67
Trade of Service - 2018			
Exports	5.769.0	111.8	1.94
Imports	5.485.0	169.5	3.09
Total Service Chain	11.254.0	281.3	2.49
Total chain of Good and Services	50.595.0	1.333.2	2.63

Source: WTO - Data compiled by the author
(1) The difference between the value exported and the value imported in the world is accounted for the lack of statistical data in some countries.

The share of African imports or exports in the interchange of goods and services of the world is not so significant if we take into account that 1.3 billion (17%) of inhabitants of the world live there. In 2018, the exports of goods in Africa accounted for only 2.45% of the exports of the world, while the imports represented just 2.88% of global imports, with a deficit of US$ 95.9 billion in the African trade balance.

As the balance of services is concerned, the situation is worse to Africans, with exports representing 1.94% against 3.09% of world imports, which accounts for a deficit of around 30% in the services trade of goods balance.

The low level of industrialization of the African continent, associated with the increase in incomes and the rapid urbanization process that takes place throughout Africa, has boosted demand for manufactured products and imposed, more and more, the need to import more of these products. In addition, it is also to consider that half of the African population is in the range from zero to 35 years, who is eager to consume digital products.

Exceeding the one trillion dollar figure in the trade interchange was an important milestone in the economic history of the African continent. This mark was surpassed in 2014 and keeps fluctuating around that number since then.

If one includes in this account the export and import of services by Africa, US$ 281.3 billion (111.8 billion in exports and 169.5 billion in imports), one we will reach more than US$ 1.3 trillion in the total trade of goods and services of Africa for the year 2018.

Achieving and exceeding the trillion-dollar mark is not a casual fact. The international trade in the African continent has been growing at quite significant rates for some time, anchored in high and sustained GDP growth rates in the vast majority of countries across the continent.

This growth trend, which repeats itself in most African countries, is due in part to the improvement of macroeconomic management in many countries and more generally to the expansion of the prices of raw materials exported by the continent, mainly oil, which provides increased payment capacity to meet the need for more imported goods and services.

Nevertheless, one has to take into account that, in several countries of the African continent, there is nowadays a wave to boost the modernization of the economy and building of institutions in many countries. This is more relevant and longer lasting than a mere rise in the commodity prices.

In the chart below one can see the growth of African exports that reached only US$ 116.8 billion in 1999, then began a steady and consistent expansion, reaching a peak of US$ 639.8 billion in 2012 and growing more than six times in that period of fewer than 10 years.

It is also possible to check the strong deleterious effect of the financial crisis that hit the world economy in 2008-2009, when the value of African exports fell more than 20%.

Merchandise trade
Exports - Africa / World
US$ billion

Source: World Trade Organization

After that, a second chock occurred with the fall in the price of the commodities in 2013, but with a recovery in the following years. The drop in commodity prices as of 2013 has led to a steeper decline in the value of exports, whose recovery has been slow and gradual since 2016.

In the other hand, the performance of total African imports, which stood around US$ 128.0 billion in 1999 was even more remarkable, once they reached US$ 573.9 billion in 2018, after a peak of US$ 642.9 billion in 2014.

Merchandise trade
Imports - Africa / World
US$ billion

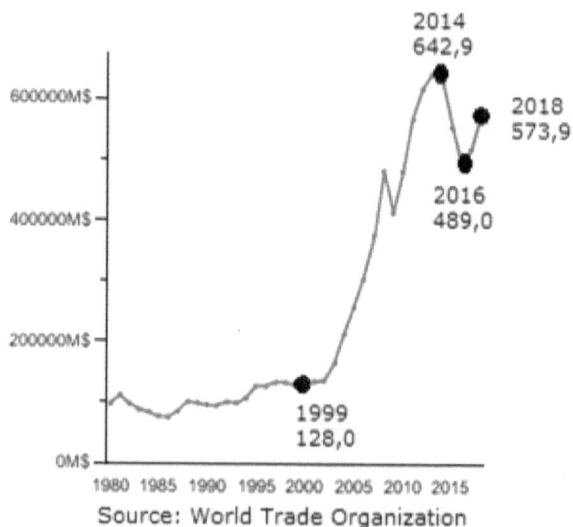

Source: World Trade Organization

Unlike exports, most of Africa's imports are manufactured goods from China, Europe and the United States of America (USA), the Africa's main trading partners.

As one can see in the graph above, the drop in commodity prices exported by the African continent (especially oil), caused a reduction in the volume of imports in 2016, but not in the same proportion as the exports in the same period. In the following years, the continent has been recovering its capacity to import.

Export of manufactured goods
Africa exports to the world
US$ billion

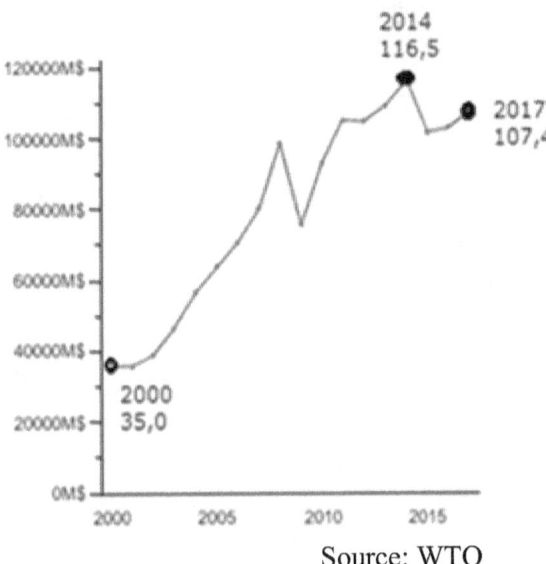

Source: WTO

Besides, a significant factor in the export agenda that is worthy to note is the growth of exports of manufactured products. Although most of the African exports are composed by oil, it is important to mention that manufactured products already compose 20% of total African exports.

As a matter of fact, exports of manufactured goods from the African continent, which was just US$ 35 billion in the year 2000, have shown strong growth, remaining above 100 billion since 2010, having reached a peak of US$ 116.5 billion in 2014.

In the same way, it is worth mentioning that there is a strong expectation of growth within some deals among African countries with the entry into force of the Continental Free Trade Agreement in July 2019. Currently, the African exports to the African countries themselves are around 18% of total exports of the African continent, while it is 50% in the Free Trade Area of Americas (FTAA) and about 70% in the European Union

The international exchanges of the African continent have grown and diversified in the last 20 years. Starting from a threshold of US$ 200 billion at the beginning of the century, it surpassed US$ 1 trillion mark in less than 20 years.

It draws attention the increasing partnership developed by China with all the countries of the African continent during that period. In 2001, imports of China from Africa were just over US$ 4.4 billion, reaching the high mark of US$ 94 billion in 2018, twenty one times more. The following table shows the development of this dynamic trade partnership.

Bilateral Commercial relationship
Africa / China in US$ billion

Africa Imports				China Exports	
Year	Total	From China	%	Total	% / Africa
2001	116.7	4.4	3.7	266.1	1.6
2018	548.5	94.1	17.1	4.494.2	2.1

China Imports				Africa Exports	
Year	Total	From Africa	%	Total	% / China
2001	243.5	3.8	1.5	113.5	3.3
2018	2.134.9	73.0	3.4	476.5	15.3

Source: ITC / TradeMap – Data compiled by author

At the beginning of the 21st century only 3.7% of African imports came from China, totaling US$ 4.4 billion, accounting for just 1.6% of Chinese exports. In 2018, this scenario changed radically: imports from China reached US$ 94 billion or 17.1% of total African imports.

On one hand, Chinese imports from Africa in 2001 were just US$ 3.8 billion, accounting for 1.5% of total Chinese imports. In 2018, this value increased to US$ 73 billion, representing 3.4% of total Chinese imports that year.

On the other hand, China accounts for 17.1% of all African imports, while Africa accounts for 15.3% of Chinese exports. The Chinese leadership in the African market, achieved in less than 20 years, consolidates its expansion year by year.

In the table below, we can see the largest exporters to the continent. In the second and distant place comes France, followed by the USA, Germany and India.

In July 2019, the Free Trade Agreement of the African continent (AfCFTA) started to operate.

Certainly, this will increase trade among South Africa and other African countries via re-exportation.

In 2018, South Africa reached the 6º place in the ranking of big exporters to African continent.

In 2004, China and the USA were both virtually tied, as the largest suppliers to the African continent, with exports around US$ 12.5 billion. Since then China has taken the lead and   been consolidating its position as the largest exporter to Africa. It is worth noting that currently the USA and France compete for the second place.

Brazil (the Atlantic neighbor) ranks seventeenth in the ranking of exporters to Africa, with just over US$ 9.3 billion in 2018. This volume of Brazilian exports is mostly due to three commodities only: sugar, meats and cereals, which together account for more than 60% of the Brazilian exports to Africa.

Main exporters to the African Continent

Exporters	Exports - US$ billion		
	2016	2017	2018
China	77.5	78.3	94.1
France	27.1	25.8	29.8
U S A	25.3	25.3	27.8
Germany	26.8	27.6	25.9
India	22.2	22.8	25.0
South Africa	**22.3**	**22.6**	**24.5**
Italy	19.2	21.6	22.1
Spain	17.9	20.3	21.1
Russian Fed.	7.3	9.5	16.7
Netherlands	11.6	11.5	16.2
Belgium	11.4	12.0	15.3
Turkey	11.9	12.2	15.0
Saudi Arabia	13.5	14.1	14.2
Korea. Republic	13.4	9.1	13.6
United Kingdom	11.0	11.3	12.0
Japan	10.7	10.3	9.9
Brazil	8.5	10.4	9.3

Source: WTO/International Trade Statistics - Data compiled by author

In the table below, of the main importers from Africa, one can see the loose leadership of China, followed by far by India, Spain, the USA and France.

Main Importers from the Africa Continent

Importers	imports – US$ billion		
	2016	2017	2018
1.China	36.8	52.2	73.0
2.India	20.6	27.0	35.3
3.Spain	18.6	23.9	30.1
4.U S A	22.4	26.2	30.0
5.France	20.7	24.9	29.5
6.Italy	17.4	20.0	24.4
7.Germany	11.3	14.4	19.8
8.Netherlands	12.1	14.9	18.2
9.U.K.	10.3	12.0	15.6
10.South Africa	13.2	13.5	14.7
11.Switzerland	11.7	11.5	12.4
12.Belgium	8.2	8.2	10.5
13.Area Nes(*)	5.6	8.2	8.1
14. South Korea	4.1	5.6	7.3
15.Japan	5.5	6.4	7.2
16.U A Emirates	16.6	16.9	6.3
17.Brazil	4.1	4.5	6.2

WTO/ International Trade Statistics – Data compiled by author
(*) Area Nes.: Not Elsewhere Specified

Supporting the African exports, the demand for more raw materials changed the scenario from 2012 onwards when China increased its imports.

With major presence and operation all over across the African continent, Chinese imports from Africa surpassed US$ 73 billion in 2018. India comes in second place with US$ 35 billion, and the USA appears in fifth place with US$ 30 billion.

Brazil ranks seventeenth in the ranking of importers from Africa, thanks mainly to imports of oil, which accounts for 90% of African exports to Brazil. Practically all navigation extant between Brazil and Africa is by vessels transporting solid or liquid bulks (oil, cereals etc.) on a port to port basis.

The high growth rates of commercial interchange (imports and exports) represent the good momentum of the African economies. When analyzing the growth of the African continent "in totum", it is possible to perceive that. Practically all African countries have grown consistently in the last 10 or 15 years.

With fifty-five countries, more than one billion inhabitants, 20% of the world's emerged lands, natural (almost) infinite riches and the poorest people of the World, Africa emerges as "the last great frontier of development" for mankind. After that only the darkness of the ocean depths or the icy whiteness of the poles.

At first glance, Africa may seem like a complicated continent to us. The wars and guerrilla warfare, which have so much hindered economic growth, have somewhat cooled down in the last five or six decades. There are remaining two or three hot spots.

Diseases such as AIDS and Ebola, however, have proved to be difficult to solve by overtaking the continent's borders and scaring the world. As much scary, as diseases are there are also the natural tragedies like prolonged droughts, which often cause starvation for thousands of people every year.

At the same time, last but not the least, it is worth to mention the lack of basic sanitation, which is one of the main vectors of disease spread. Even with all these adversities, there is the emergence of a new Africa, of a "new" economic dynamics throughout the African continent in the first two decades of the current twenty-first century.

African societies are democratizing themselves in search of political and administrative transparency. Processes that are more modern are replacing old-fashioned production methods. Agriculture has responded satisfactorily to the introduction of new technologies and the youth have looked to the future with more confidence.

Certainly, there are huge pockets of poverty scattered across the continent, desolate areas and a large portion of population living below the poverty line. However, the main economic indicators point to the gradual reduction of these old problems in Africa.

In contrast with all these bad news, several countries grew more than five percent, with some growing over seven or eight percent a year. Even poorer countries, such as Niger, with all sorts of hardships that one can imagine, have grown steadily over 4% a year, reaching better levels of social and economic development in the whole of African continent.

The worsening and expansion of the Ebola virus on the African West Coast in 2013 created enormous economic problems for the entire region, with some isolation from the international community, even in cases where drastic reduction of Ebola virus contamination were reported.

The disparity of income, regional and interregional, is another factor that draws attention. Most African countries are in the range of up to US$ 1.000 per capita income, with Malawi, Burundi and the Central African Republic standing at less than US$ 400 per year.

The vast majority of countries are in the range of up to US$ 5.000 per capita income. Few are in the range of up to US$ 10.000 and still less in the range of over US$ 10.000, standing out in the tip Equatorial Guinea, with US$ 20.000 of annual per capita income.

Certainly, there are difficulties, but if Africans and South Americans fail to face these problems upfront, they will never "reach" the goal of transforming the South Atlantic into our bridge, into our connecting element.

Chapter III
The multilateral trade of South America

In South America, before the arrival of Europeans, long trails already connected the peoples of the whole continent.

The Brazilian territory, since the discovery by the Portuguese in 1500, showed to the first settlers a lot of riches, beginning with the *Pau Brazil* (a kind of red wood). This also aroused interest of other colonizers, like the French; the British, the Dutch, and the Spaniards. There was also another kind of stakeholders: the buccaneers and pirates.

All these actors, in one way or another, tried to establish themselves in the Portuguese South America, whether by force of arms or by slow invasion, purely and simply. The Netherlands occupied the so called "Dutch Brazil", in the present state of Pernambuco, and also the Dutch Guiana (today Suriname), whose capital is Paramaribo, and some islands in the Caribbean.

France invaded and took possession of the region where today is the city of Rio de Janeiro in 1555. The so-called France Antarctica (as the region was named) endured just for a few years. The Portuguese expelled them in 1560 and then founded the city of Rio de Janeiro.

The French invaded other areas in Brazilian territory, but the most remarkable one was in 1612 when they founded the city of São Luís, now the capital of the present state of Maranhão. The "invasion" that was denominated "Equinoctial France" lasted only three years. They were put away from São Luís in 1615.

After the failed invasions into Brazil, the French occupied a region more to the North, the French Guiana (now an overseas department of France whose capital is Cayenne). In French Guiana it is located the rocket launching base of Khouru.

The British, in turn, after many attempts, managed to keep the occupation of the English Guiana (today only Guyana whose capital is Georgetown), and some other territories in the Caribbean.

Finally, Spain, which respecting the Treaty of Tordesillas[6] took possession of lands beyond the 370 leagues west of Cape Verde and dominated the entire western part of South America and dozens of other territories in the Caribbean.

For better or for worse, South America survived the colonial period and today with 12 countries, 17.8 million square kilometers, and 420 million people is among the major geo-economic areas of the World. The continent has huge mineral and agricultural productions and a diversified manufacturing industry.

In the tables below it is possible to check the share of South America in the global trade market.

---

[6] *The Treaty of Tordesillas, signed between Portugal and Spain in 1494, stipulated that all lands discovered and to be discovered up to 370 leagues (around 2,200 km) to the west of Cape Verde should belong to Portugal. Meanwhile, the lands discovered beyond that limit should belong to Spain.*

Importers in S. America – US$ million

Importers	2016	2017	2018
World	16.041.4	17.795.0	19.665.2
South America	394.2	431.1	486.8
S.A in world %	2.4%	2.4%	2.5%
Brazil	137.5	150.7	181.2
Chile	59.3	65.2	74.1
Argentina	55.9	66.8	65.4
Colombia	44.8	46.0	51.2
Peru	36.1	39.7	43.1
Ecuador	16.1	19.8	23.0
Paraguay	9.7	11.8	13.3
Venezuela	15.5	10.5	11.2
Bolivia	8.5	9.3	9.9
Uruguay	8.1	8.4	9.0
Guyana	1.6	1.7	3.9
Suriname	1.1	1.2	1.5

Source: ITC – Trademap – Data compiled by author

The total imports of South America reached the mark of US$ 529 billion in 2018, which accounts for 2.89% of global imports. Brazil, as the biggest importer in South America, imported US$ 181 billion, or 34% of total imports by South America (little less than 1% of global imports), followed by Chile with 13.4% and Argentina with 12.3%

Exporters in South America – US$ million

Exporters	2016	2017	2018
World	15.881.8	17.550.8	19.284.5
South America	442.1	505.2	550.6
S.A in the world %	2.8%	2.9%	2.8%
Brazil	185.2	217.7	239.8
Chile	60.7	68.8	75.4
Argentina	57.8	58.3	61.5
Peru	36.3	44.0	47.2
Colombia	31.0	37.7	41.7
Venezuela	29.3	32.0	35.0
Ecuador	16.7	19.1	21.6
Paraguay	8.5	8.6	9.0
Bolivia	7.1	8.1	8.9
Uruguay	6.9	7.8	7.6
Suriname	1.2	1.4	1.5
Guyana	1.4	1.7	1.4

Source: ITC – Trademap – Data compiled by author

The total exports of South America reached US$ 556 billion in 2018, which represents 2.88% of the global exports. Brazil is also the biggest exporter in South America with exports of US$ 239 billion, which accounts for 42.9% of total exports from South America. Chile and Argentina complete the triad with 13% and 11%, respectively.

The continent's trade balance presents some equilibrium, with South America's sharing something like 2.9% of the global market in both sides.

However, in terms of the balance of trade of services, the same trend that happens in Africa also applies to South America: a permanent deficit. Services, such as transport, tourism, finances, communication; consulting etc., are deficit-ridden in both Africa and South America.

All the value of imports and exports are "overtaxed" around 10% only on the transport item. If a given country has no transportation companies to balance this account, one can say that at least 10% of its import/export earnings are swallowed in the balance of services.

The new deal for the South Atlantic, proposed by this book has as focus the maritime transport between South America and West Africa. Of course, if we manage to find the solution for the transport issue, we will be opening the way not only to have more trade in goods but also to a series of more services, increasing thereby the sources of income of all the SARIS[7] countries.

The SARIS, is a "non-official" economic block, comprehending the countries bathed by South Atlantic, and participating in the Zone of Peace and Cooperation of South Atlantic – ZPCAS - Agreement.

This agreement, named also as ZOPACAS, were signed in 1986 by the three countries in South America and by the 22 countries partners in Atlantic Africa.

In Chapter VII will explain better the idea of the South Atlantic Regional Integration System – SARIS.

---

[7] *SARIS is the abbreviation for the South Atlantic Regional Integration System. A system linking countries on both sides of the South Atlantic.*

Chapter IV
The commercial relationship between Africa and South America

The Atlantic Ocean can be a meek and calm creek or a brave and troubled sea.

Everything depends on the intention of the governments of the countries that border it

The colonization of the Americas began shortly after the Europeans started to explore the West Coast of the African continent. The slave labor was brought from Africa to work hard to produce in the Americas the goods and extract raw materials that were widely demanded throughout Europe.

With South America, mainly Brazil, it could not be different. About Brazil, Pero Vaz de Caminha[8], the registrar of fleet captain Pedro Álvares Cabral, wrote: *"Those lands are so fertile that in planting everything grows"*.

In the same way, the Europeans that adventured themselves through that vast landmass used to say: *"The place where diamonds and emeralds sprouted out of the land in abundance never seen"*.

The basis of the economy of the settlements of the "new world" was found on agricultural and in mineral and vegetable extraction. The slave labor became more necessary than ever. The slave labor force was widely used throughout America thereby constituting the cornerstone of agricultural, mining and all other sectors of the economy.

It is estimated that approximately 10 million Africans were forcibly transported as slaves to Brazil and other areas of South America over three centuries. Today Brazil is a kind of big African country outside Africa.

---

[8] *In the letter of the "discovery" of Brazil, written to Dom Manuel, King of Portugal, in May of 1500.*

Therefore, by our common history, by the bonds of blood that unite us, by geographical proximity and by the tradition to develop business, South America and Africa had a good share in the international trade of the world at that period.

Two or three centuries ago, nothing could happen on one side of the Atlantic that did not spilled over the other. However, what can be checked nowadays is a very low share in this bilateral trade, not exceeding 3% of total demands on both sides.

What happened in the past and what is happening with our economic relationship? Why import from or export to Africa is so difficult to do now?

To understand the commercial relationship between South America and Africa better, one had rather to consider the interaction of the economic blocks on both sides that cover all countries bathed by the South Atlantic Ocean.

These blocks are the Mercosur in South America and ECOWAS, CEMAC/UDEAC and SADC in the African side.

Argentina, Brazil, Paraguay and Uruguay founded the Common Market of the South (Mercosur) in 1991. Venezuela joined the group in 2013; however, it was suspended for breaking the democratic clause of the agreement.

The Mercosur covers all the Atlantic side of South America from Patagonia up to beyond the Equator line.

The same way, the three Atlantic African blocks, the Economic Community of West Africa States (ECOWAS), the Central African Economic and Monetary Community (CEMAC) and Southern Africa Development Countries (SADC) cover all side of Africa bathed by the Atlantic Ocean starting from South Africa up to Senegal.

The Mercosur accounts for 72% of South America territory (11.8 million km^2); 61.9% of the population (around 262 million inhabitants); with a GDP of US$ 2.6 trillion, that represents two thirds of the GDP of South America in 2018, according to the International Monetary Fund (IMF).

Basic data: Mercosur - 2018

Block	Population Million	Territory 1000 Km2	GDP US$ Billion
Mercosur	262.2	11.874.1	2.628.0
S. America	423.7.5	17.722.4	3.606.2
% S. America	61.9	67.0	72.9

Source: IBGE / Mercosur web site.

Mercosur does business with almost all countries in the world. Notwithstanding, the main trade partners are China, Europe, USA, Japan and Korea. Inside the block, Brazil is the big partner of all other Mercosur countries. In the table below one can see the main trade connections of Mercosur countries.

Commercial partnership/ Mercosur– 2018

Countries		Partners				
Brazil	Imports	EU	US	CH	ARG	KOR
	Exports	CHI	EU	US	ARG	JP
ARG	Imports	BRA	CHI	EU	US	MX
	Exports	BRA	EU	US	CHI	KOR
URU	Imports	CHI	BRA	EU	ARG	US
	Exports	BRA	EU	CHI	US	ARG
PAR	Imports	CHI	BRA	ARG	EU	US
	Exports	BRA	EU	ARG	RU	CHIL

Source: ITC – Trademap – Data compiled by author

China is a major partner of all Mercosur countries in either importing or exporting. The same happens in Africa, where China becomes increasingly a more important partner selling to or buying from Africa.

This partnership between South America and Africa with China is rather recent. Twenty years ago, China was not among the ten most important players in importing or exporting sectors from both continents. As Africa continent is concerned, the aggregation of the three Atlantic blocks has the following characteristics.

Basic data: ECOWAS/CEMAC/SADC -2018

Blocks	Population million	Territory 1000 Km^2	GDP US$ billion
ECOWAS	377.4	5,112.0	614.9
CEMAC	50.2	3,018.0	194.3
SADC	355.4	9,871.4	716.6

Total blocks	783.1	18,001.4	1,425.8
Total Africa	1,245.9	30,300.0	2,088,1
% / Africa	62.8%	59.4%	68.3%

Source: IMF; Economic blocks web sites.

Among the sovereign countries bordering the South Atlantic, there are three in South America plus twenty-two in Africa. The total population of these countries reaches more than one billion inhabitants, 30.3 million square kilometers and a combined GDP close to four trillion dollars.

That is the size of the economic region of the South Atlantic, which is a major market by any comparison indicator one can use. This market will be from now on denominated as South Atlantic Regional Integration System (SARIS).

Basic data of SARIS - 2018

Block	Population million	Territory 1000 Km²	GDP/PPP US$ billion
MERCOSUR	263.6	11,874.1	2.488.8
ECOWAS	377,4	5,112.0	614.9
CEMAC	50,2	3,018.0	194.3
SADC	355.4	9,871.4	716.9
TOTAL	1,046.6	29,875.5	4,014.9

Source: IMF; Web sites of each block. Data compiled by author

Those two large markets, face to face, combine a US$ 4.0 trillion GDP. It is worth asking how are the business links between these continental blocks connected by the South Atlantic.

The trade volume between the bordering countries of South Atlantic Ocean represents less than 3% (three) of the total trade of each other. In addition, primary commodities compose most of all trade.

There are complementary economies in both sides but it is too difficult to realize deals because of the virtual absence of transport lines between them.

Despite the natural difficulties and the nonexistence of maritime transport lines, the bilateral trade has been growing. Of course, the majority deals are concentrated on commodity products, such as oil, sugar, meat, cereals, fertilizers and others that account for around 70% of the total of the trade. This kind of product is transported not in containers; they usually go in the holds of ships.

As manufactured products are loaded in containers, the difficulties come up. The need for transshipment in Europa or in South Africa, the navigation time and the cost of the freight erode the competitiveness of the products of both sides of the Atlantic Ocean.

Whenever I am visiting the African continent I perceive clearly the bonds that bring us closer, as if both sides were there just waiting for an opportunity to do business. Unfortunately, however, the difficulties always arise.

Following will see the commerce between Mercosur and each one of the blocks in Africa and in the sequence the consolidate data of this big market (not so big yet).

The commerce Mercosur / ECOWAS

Mercosur imports from ECOWAS US$ million				
Importers	2016	2017	2018	% 2018
MERCOSUR	2,189.5	1,804.3	2,490.9	-----
Brazil	1,542.6	1,102.8	1,838.9	73.8
Uruguay	238.6	197.6	353.4	14.1
Argentina	407.9	503.2	298.2	11.9

Mercosur export to ECOWAS – US$ million				
Exporters	2016	2017	2018	% 2018
MERCOSUR	1,693.7	2,008.0	2,057.3	------
Brazil	1,448.2	1,623.7	1,596.0	77.6
Argentina	178.4	286.9	374.4	18.2
Uruguay	36.3	60.2	45.8	2.2
Paraguay	8.8	18.4	12.0	0.6

Source: ITC /Trade MAP – Data compiled by the author

In the tables above, one can check the volume and composition of the trade between the economic blocks of Mercosur, in South America, and ECOWAS, CEMAC and SADC on the African side.

The ECOWAS is one of the big economic blocks in Africa. There are 15 countries, with population over 377.4 million of inhabitants and GDP over US$ 614.9 billion. The biggest economy of the region is Nigeria, a great exporter of oil.

Mercosur has developed a strong relationship with ECOWAS. The imports by Mercosur reached US$ 2.5 billion in 2018, compared to little more than US$ 2.0 billion of exports from Mercosur to ECOWAS.

Brazil shares more than 70% of the total trade with that block. In imports, the share of   Brazil reaches 73.8%. Meanwhile, in terms of exports from Mercosur to ECOWAS, the Brazilian share is 77.6%. Argentina and Uruguay are significant in that deal, reaching, sometimes, about 20% of either total imported or exported. Paraguay (a landlocked country) has its natural difficulties in logistic but is also an active partner.

In the table below it possible to verify the main product on both sides of the trade and the main importers and exporters to each product.

Main products imported by Mercosur from ECOWAS in 2018 – US$ million

HS code	US$ million	%	Main supplier In Ecowas	Main buyer In Mercsur
All products	2,490.9	100 %	In Ecowas	In Mercsur
27 Mineral fuels and oils	2,104.7	84.5	Nigeria $2,104.7	Brazil $1,493.2
				Uruguay $ 342.8
31 Fertilizers	167.9	6.7	Nigeria $ 158.8	Brazil $ 134.4
			Senegal $ 9.1	Argentina $ 25.5
18 Cocoa	155.6	6.2	Ghana $ 136.6	Brazil $ 153.3
			C. dIvoire $ 18.7	Uruguay $ 2.1
40 Rubber and articles thereof	34.7	1.4	C. dIvoire $ 31.5	Brazil $ 30.9
			Guinea $ 2.0	Argentina $ 3.7
08 Edible fruit and nuts	12.0	0.5	C. dIvoire $ 8.8	Brazil $ 12.0
			G. Bissau $ 1.7	

Source: ITC /Trade MAP – Data compiled by the author

In 2018, the total of imports by Mercosur from ECOWAS reached US$ 2.490.9 million. The Oil (petroleum HS-27) sales were responsible for US$ 2.104.7 million that represents 84.5% of the total imports by Mercosur from ECOWAS.

The great and single exporter of petroleum in ECOWAS is Nigeria. The main buyers in Mercosur are also concentrated. Brazil imports more than 70% of the total imported by Mercosur, followed by Uruguay with 16.3%.

Fertilizers (HS-31), the second main product, are supplied by Nigeria, with 94.6% of the total exported to Mercosur and followed by Senegal. The main buyers in Mercosur are Brazil, with 80.2% of the total imported, and Argentina.

Cocoa (HS-18), the third product, is supplied by Ghana, with 87.8% of total exported, and Côte d´Ivoire. The main buyers in Mercosur are Brazil, with 98.7% of the total imported by Mercosur.

In fourth place comes Rubber (HS-40), whose main supplier in ECOWAS is Côte d´Ivoire, with 91.1% of total. In Mercosur, the main buyers are Brazil (88.2%) and Argentina.

Côte d´Ivoire is also the main supplier of Edible Fruits and Nuts (HS-08), with 73.3%, followed by Guinea Bissau. Brazil is the unique buyer of this product in Mercosur.

On the realm of exports from Mercosur to ECOWAS, the range of products is more diversified than imports and reaches the mark of US$ 2.057 million.

The first product exported is sugar, which accounts for 38% of the total exported from Mercosur to ECOWAS. Brazil responds with almost 100% of sugar export to Africa, while Nigeria is responsible for at least 50% of imports. Benin occupies the second place, with 17% of the imports of sugar.

Main products exported by Mercosur to ECOWAS - 2018

Product HS code	Value US$ million	%	Main supplier	Main buyer
All products	2,057.3	100%	In Mercosur	In ECOWAS
17 - Sugars and sugar confectionery	790.9	38.4	Brazil 790.9	Nigeria 387.3 Benin 132.6
10 Cereals	320.7	15.6	Argentina 164.5 Brazil 126.2	Snegal 136.5 Nigeria 58.6
87 Vehicles other than railway	161.8	7.8	Brazil 161.8	Nigeria 131.1 Ghana 25.9
27 Mineral fuels and mineral oils	151.9	7.6	Brazil 102.4	Liberia 99.7 Nigeria 20.8
02 Meat and edible meat	95.8	4.7	Brazil 91.9 Argentina 3.1	Niger 26.9 Ghana 24.0

Source: ITC /Trade MAP – Data compiled by the author

The second product exported by Mercosur to ECOWAS are Cereals, which account for 15% of the total exports. The main buyer in ECOWAS is Senegal, with 42.5%, followed by Nigeria, with 18.1%. The main supplier is Argentina, with 51.2%, and Brazil with 39.4%.

The third product is Vehicles (HS-87), which reaches US$ 161 million. The single exporter is Brazil, while the biggest importer in ECOWAS is Nigeria, with 81.4%, followed by Ghana with 15.5%.

The exports of Mineral Fuels (HS-27) reaches US$ 151.9 million. Brazil is the main supplier with 67.5%. The buyers in ECOWAS are Liberia, with 66%, followed by Nigeria with 13.6%.

Meat (HS-02) is the fifth export product from Mercosur to ECOWAS. Brazil exports 95.6%, followed by Argentina with 3.2%. In ECOWAS the main importer are Niger, with 28.1%, followed by Ghana with 25%.

The commerce Mercosur x CEMAC

Mercosur Imports from CEMAC – US$ million			
Importers	2016	2017	2018
MERCOSUR	$ 168.7	$ 232.3	$ 33.4
Argentina	$ 14.4	$ 148.7	$ 22.7
Brazil	$ 147.3	$ 83.2	$ 10.3
Uruguay	$ 6.9	$ 2	$ 1
Paraguay			$ 1
Mercosur Export to CEMAC – US$ million			
Exporters	2016	2017	2018
MERCOSUR	$ 195.0	$ 242.4	$ 225.7
Brazil	$ 128.5	$ 151.6	$ 136.8
Argentina	$ 46.7	$ 66.5	$ 60.7
Uruguay	$ 12.4	$ 13.9	$ 18.3
Paraguay	$ 7.3	$ 10.2	$ 9.7

Source: ITC /Trade MAP – Data compiled by the author

The CEMAC has only six member countries: Equatorial Guinea, Cameroun, Gabon, Centro-African Republic, Congo Republic and Chad. The population is 50.3 million of inhabitants and the combined GDP under US$ 94.3 billion.

Beyond this "little numbers" though, the CEMAC has two countries with the highest per capita GDP of Africa: Equatorial Guinea (US$ 21,3 thousand) and Gabon (US$ 19,0), according to Monetary International Found – IMF.

Mercosur and CEMAC have certain instability in their bilateral trade relationship, exhibiting volatility especially in imports. In 2018, the imports were only US$ 22 million after a peak of US$ 232 million in 2017. The main importer from CEMAC in 2018 was Argentina, with US$ 22.7 million, following Brazil with US$ 10 million.

In the exports side, the trade is more stable, with exports oscillating around US$ 200 million per year. In 2018, the exports from Mercosur to CEMAC reached US$ 225.7 million. Brazil is the main exporter, having sold goods in the amount of US$ 136.8 million to CEMAC in 2018, followed by Argentina, with US$ 60.7 million, and Uruguay with US$ 18.7 million.

Main products imported by Mercosur from CEMAC in 2018 – US$ million

HS code	Value total US$ million	%	Main supplier	Main buyer
All products	33.4	100 %	In CEMAC	In Mercosur
27 Mineral fuels.	21.8	65.2	E. Guinea 21.8	Argentina 21.8
29 Organic chemicals	8.5	25.4	E. Guinea 8.5	Brazil 8.5
44 Wood	1.4	4.2	Gabon 0.7 Cameroun 0.6	Argentina 0.9 Brazil 0.3
18 Cocoa	1.2	3.5	Cameroun 1.2	Brazil 1.2
84 Machinery	0.1	0.2	E. Guinea 0.1	Paraguay 0.1

Source: ITC /Trade MAP – Data compiled by the author

After a peak of US$ 232 million in 2017, total imports of Mercosur from CEMAC went down to US$ 33.4 million in 2018. This occurred because Argentina in economic crisis reduced its imports of petroleum.

By the way, Petroleum accounts for 65.4% of imports of Mercosur from CEMAC. Argentina is the single importer in Mercosur. The single supplier of this product in CEMAC is Equatorial Guinea.

The second main important item in this bilateral trade is the complex of Organic Chemicals (HS–29). The main supplier is Equatorial Guinea and the main buyer in Mercosur is Brazil. Wood and

Articles of Wood (HS–44) occupy the third place in this market, being Gabon and Cameroon the main suppliers. Argentina and Brazil are the main buyers in Mercosur.

For Cocoa and Cocoa Preparations (HS-18), Cameroun is the main supplier, while Brazil is the single buyer in Mercosur. With regards to Machinery and Mechanical Appliances (HS-84), Equatorial Guinea is main supplier, while Paraguay is the main buyer in Mercosur.

Main products exported by Mercosur to CEMAC in 2018 – US$ million

Product HS code	US$ million	%	Main supplier	Main buyer
All products	225.7	100%	In Mercosur	In CEMAC
02 - Meat and edible meat offal	63.4	28.1	Brazil 48.0 Paraguay 8.7	Gabon 32.7 Congo 20.6
28 Inorganic organic chemicals	42.8	18.9	Brazil 42.8	Cameroon 42.8
03 - Fish, crustaceans. mollusks and other aquatic	35.8	15.8	Uruguay 17.3 Argentina 15.8	Cameroon 18.3 Gabon 11.4
23 Residues and waste from the food industries;	22.1	9.8	Argentina 21.5	Cameroon 21.5
17 Sugars and confectionery	8.3	3.7	Brazil 8.3	Cameroon 6.7 E. Guinea 1.1

Source: ITC – Trademap – Data compiled by author

In addition, the exports from Mercosur to CEMAC reached US$ 225.7 million in 2018. The main product exported was Meat and Edible Meat (HS-02), with 28.1% of the total exported by Mercosur. The main suppliers in Mercosur were Brazil and Paraguay, while the main buyer in CEMAC are Gabon, with 51.6%, and Congo with 32.5%.

Inorganic Chemicals (HS-28) occupy the second place, with 18.9% of exports from Mercosur. The main and single supplier is Brazil and the main and single buyer is Cameroon. Fish and Crustaceans (HS-03) occupy the third place in this trade, with 15.8% of total exported. Uruguay, with 48.3%, and Argentina, with 44.1%, are the main exporters in Mercosur. Cameroon, with 51.1%, and Gabon, with 31.8%, are the main importers in CEMAC.

As to Food Industry (HS-23), Argentina and Cameroon are the main and single exporters and importers, being responsible for 9.8% of total trade between Mercosur and CEMAC. The fifth most important product is Sugar (HS-17) that represents 3.7% of total trade, being Brazil the main and single exporter, while Cameroun, with 80.7%, and Equatorial Guinea, with 13.2%, are the main buyers in CEMAC.

The third block, SADC is the biggest economic block in Africa. Comprised of 15 countries with a population of over 355.4 million people and a GDP of over US$ 716.9 billion (in 2018). SADC is led by South Africa, the most developed country in Africa.

The trade interchange between Mercosur and SADC is higher than US$ 4.5 billion, engaging all the countries and a variety of products.

The commerce Mercosur x SADC

Importers from SADC – US$ million			
Importers	2016	2017	2018
MERCOSUR	948.5	1.171.1	1.728.1
Brazil	463.8	915.6	1.100.1
Uruguay	249.0	27.9	384.0
Argentina	208.8	206.6	221.1
Paraguay	13.4	16.3	14.1
Exporters to SADC – US$ million			
Exporters	2016	2017	2018
MERCOSUR	3.328.0	3.259.8	2.792.6
Brazil	2.163.7	2.445.6	1.966.4
Argentina	1.008.7	737.7	752.9
Uruguay	28.7	35.5	40.9
Paraguay	110.9	18.4	23.9

Source: ITC – Trademap – Data compiled by author

The imports by Mercosur from SADC reaches US$ 1.7 billion. See table below. The main product imported is the Mineral fuels and Mineral Oils (HS-27), with US$ 815 million that represents 47% of all imports. The main suppliers in SADC are Angola, with 70%, and Mozambique. In Mercosur, Brazil accounts for 52.3% of imports, followed by Uruguay.

The second product in the trade interchange is Precious and Semi-precious Stones (HS-71), which reached US$ 141.8 million in 2018. The main and single supplier in SADC is South Africa, while the main buyer in Mercosur is Brazil. The third most important product is Aluminum and articles thereof (HS-76) whose imports reached US$123.5 million in 2018. The main and single supplier is South Africa, while the main buyer in Mercosur is Brazil, with 95.9%, followed by Argentina.

Main products imported by Mercosur from SADC in 2018 – US$ million

Product HS code	Value total	%	Main supplier In SADC	Main buyer In Mercosur
All products	1.728.1	100%		
27 Mineral fuels, oils, and products of their distillation	815.0	47.2	Angola 571.6 Mozambiq 129.9	Brazil 431.0 Uruguay 361.8
71 pearls, or semi-precious stones	141.8	8.2	S. Africa 141.7	Brazil 137.4
76 - Aluminium and articles thereof	123.5	7.1	S. Africa 122.4	Brazil 118.6 Argentina 4.9
72 Iron and steel	95.3	5.5	S. Africa 94.3	Brazil 69.9 Argentina 24.0
74 Copper and articles thereof	73.9	4.3	DRC 59.0 Zambia 14.1	Brazil 73.2

Source: ITC – Trademap – Data compiled by author

Iron and Steel rank in the fourth place with imports around US$ 95.3 million. The main and single supplier in SADC is South Africa. The main buyers in Mercosur are Brazil, with 73.7% of imports, and Argentina with 25.2%. In the fifth place comes Copper and Articles thereof, whose imports reached US$ 73.9 million, with the main suppliers in SADC being the Democratic Republic of Congo (DRC) with 79.7%, and Zambia with 19%. In Mercosur, Brazil is the single buyer of that product.

The exports from Mercosur to SADC reached US$ 2,792.6 billion in 2018. The five main products traded and the main suppliers and buyers are as follows.

Main products exported by Mercosur to SADC 2018

Product HS code	US$ million	%	Main supplier	Main buyer
All products	2.792.6	100 %	In Mercosur	In SADC
02 - Meat and edible meat offal	524.5	18.7	Brazil 470.3 Argentina 167.0	S. Africa 319.7 Angola 167.0
87 - Vehicles other than railway	434.1	15.5	Brazil 297.7 Argentina 135.9	S. Africa 380.4 Angola 43.9
23 - Residues and waste from the food	185.4	6.6	Argentina 161.1 Brazil 14.0	S. Africa 173.9 Angola 5.3
84 - Machinery. mechanical appliances	179.3	6.4	Brazil 166.9 Argentina 12.2	S. Africa 142.0 Angola 14.8
17 Sugars and sugar confection	163.6	5.8	Brazil 163.6	Angola 104.7 S. Africa 40.3

Source: ITC – Trademap – Data compiled by author

The main product in the export basket is Meat and Edible Meat (HS-02), which occupy 18.7% of exports. The main exporters are Brazil, with 89.7% of exports, and Argentina with 9.1%. The main buyers in SADC are South Africa, with 60.9% of imports, followed by Angola with 31.2%. The main importers in SADC are South Africa, whose imports account for 60.9% of total, followed by Angola with 31.8% of total imports.

The second product is Vehicles (HS-87) amounting US$ 434.1 million (15.5% of total imports). Brazil is the main exporter, with 68.6%, followed by Argentina with 31.3%. These two countries are the only exporters of vehicles from Mercosur to SADC. Meanwhile, in SADC, the main buyers are South Africa, with 87.5%, followed by Angola with 10.1% of total imports.

Residues and Waste of Food Industry (HS-23) are the third group of products mostly imported by SADC from Mercosur, having reached the mark of US$ 185.4 million. Argentina is the main exporter, with 87.0% of exports, followed by far by Brazil. with 7.6% of total exports. The main importer in SADC is South Africa with 94.1%, followed by Angola with 2.8% of total imports.

Machinery (HS-84) with total imports of US$ 179.3 million is the fourth group of main products imported by SADC from Mercosur. The main exporter is Brazil with 93% of the total, followed by Argentina, with 6.7% of total imports of Machinery. In SADC, 79.3% of these products are imported by South Africa, followed by Angola with 8.2% of total imports.

Sugar (HS-17) is the fifth product mostly imported by SADC with value of $ 163.6 million. Brazil is the unique exporter. Angola buys 63.8% of the imports, followed by South Africa with 24.5% of total imports of sugar.

In the table below, one can see the consolidated numbers of the trade interchange between Mercosur, in South America, and the three above-mentioned economic blocks scattered through the West Coast of Africa.

Trade interchange between Mercosur and the three combined economic blocks in the Atlantic Africa: ECOWAS, CEMAC and SADC. Value in US$ million.

Importers	2016	2017	2018
MERCOSUR	3.306.7	3.207.7	4.252.4
Brazil	2.153.7	1.101.6	2.949.3
Uruguay	494.5	225.7	737.5
Argentina	631.1	858.5	542.0
Paraguay	13.5	16.4	14.3
Exporters	2016	2017	2018
MERCOSUR	5.216.7	5.510.2	5.075.6
Brazil	3.740.4	4.220.9	1.732.8
Argentina	1.233.8	1.091.1	1.188.0
Uruguay	77.4	109.6	105.0
Paraguay	127.0	47.0	45.6

Source: ITC – Data compiled by author

The trade interchange (Import + export) between South America (Mercosur) and Africa (Atlantic side) reached over US$ 9.3 million in 2018. Brazil is the biggest player in South America (Mercosur), with a trade interchange of US$ 4.6 billion. Argentina comes in second with US$ 1.9 billion. The majority of the products dealt are primary products (commodities) with low value added. Those products account for more than 70% of the value traded.

Manufactured and/or semi-manufactured products, which add more value during the manufacturing process represent less than 30% of the total value of trade between Mercosur and the three economic blocks in Africa. The lack of appropriate maritime transportation and the natural difficulties resulting from this fact make the business extremely difficulty to be made between these two continental blocks.

Despite that, products such as Footwear and Furniture (HS-64) made in Brazil are found in many African countries and African-made fabrics are easily found in Brazil and Argentina. Footwear, gaiters and the like; parts of such articles (HS-64) produced in Brazil meet a firm demand over $ 20 million per year in Africa.

US$ thousand

64	Footwear, gaiters and the like; parts of such articles	24.771	21.970	22.732

Source: ITC – Trademap

Clothes and Other Similar Articles (HS-62), manufactured in Africa, are enough demanded in Brazil. These products find growing demand in South America. In 2018, the importation reached over $ 4 million.

US$ thousand

62	Articles of apparel and clothing accessories. not knitted or crocheted	839	1.634	4.172

Source: ITC – Trademap

The introduction of a fast and cheap maritime transport can raise the level of changes between these two continental blocks in a short space of time. Actually, at least US$ 2 billion are dealt between Africa and South America with manufactured or semi-manufactured products. Such volume of merchandise generates a reasonable volume of containers making a stop in Europe before arriving in their final destination. These containers could be crossing the South Atlantic without the need to make a stop in Europe.

Three or four ports in South America and three or four ports in Africa could be chosen to serve as hub ports on both sides. The navigation on coast waters service could complete the way to minor ports.

Chapter V
The effects of **Suez** and **Panama** Channels all over navigation on South Atlantic

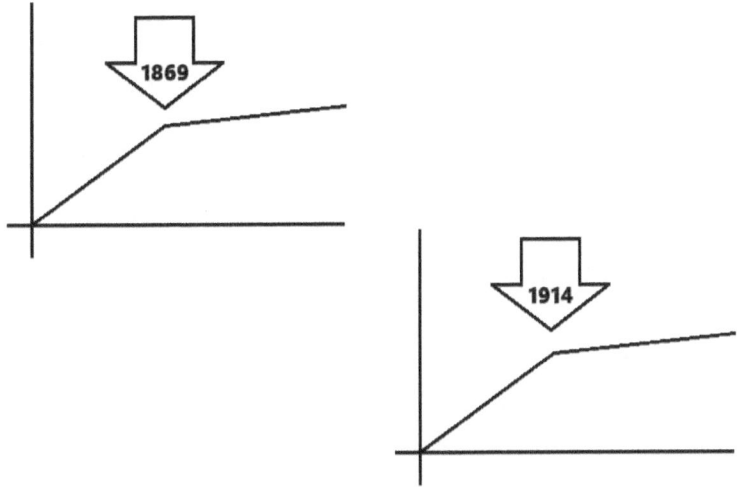

For thousands of years men dreamed of running like the animals, swim like the fishes and fly like the birds.

Problems of various kinds and dreams of different natures have always arisen in the way of the progress of humanity. For all and for every one of the dreams dreamed or the problems arisen, man created or invented a means of resolving them. The solution could be bypassing them, passing over them or passing through them.

Researching for a solution to the troubles, or to realize their dreams, the men run more than animals, sails more than fishes and flies more than birds. The great majority of human inventions to solve the problems encountered brought benefits to all humankind. However, some inventions, such as instruments of torture and weapons of mass destruction have only brought death, sadness and pain to an individual either alone or to an entire country or community.

Certain inventions or creations have privileged some societies or brought great development to one region over others. It is about these activities that we are going to talk now. The nineteenth century was especially beneficial for world economic growth, mainly for European countries because of the beginning and consolidation of the industrial revolution. In the same way, the USA was creating the basis to emerging as pretender of the first place in the world economy.

Until the eighteenth century, most of the products consumed by societies used to come from artisanal activity. The artisans had complete control on the productive process. The vast majority of the European population lived in the countryside and practically produced their own consumption. In the larger cities of Britain and France, there were already the so-called "manufactures", which were factories without machines only with artisanal workers where each one took care to produce its product.

Introduction of the machines in the production process provoked a revolution in the labour relations, thereby virtually eliminating the artisanal work and allowed for the mass production in several sectors to emerge. Moreover, of course, it increased the use of raw materials to meet the new way of consumption.

The expansion of shipping routes and the existence of raw materials, plentiful in Africa, South America and Asia have pushed industrial production to the pinnacle of unprecedented growth.

In the first phase of the industrial era, the mass production process was almost exclusive to Britain, which, in turn, also had the largest merchant fleet of that time. At the beginning of the 19th century, from 1820 onwards, other European countries, such as Germany, France; Austria; Belgium etc. began introducing machines into their production processes in a big scale.

Therefore, the countries of South America. Africa and Asia became important suppliers of raw materials, both agricultural and mineral, for the development of the industry that was growing in Europe and the United States. Parallel to economic growth, the nautical industry was developing with ships becoming bigger, faster and of greater autonomy.

Based on industry, especially the textile industry, Europe's trade with the rest of the world has grown considerably, turning Europe and the United States into the "engines" of world economic development. The navigation between Europe and Asia was made circumventing the **Cape of Good Hope,** at the tip of Africa or by the **Strait of Magellan,** at the extreme point of the South American continent. To go and come back there demanded a long time.

The other and first way between Europe and Asia was the "silk route" used centuries and centuries ago. However, this was not a good idea because of the time expended in the journey, much more then circumventing the **Cape of Good Hope** in Africa or **Magellan strait** in South America.

The African route envisaged stopovers in Senegal, Benin, Nigeria, Angola etc. and to Cape town, which was the last stop on the Atlantic side. After rounding the Cape of Good Hope, the first stop in the Indian Ocean was in Durban, both cities in current South Africa.

On the Europe/Africa/Asia route, going or coming, the scale in South Africa and in several other ports was obligatory. The vessels had not autonomy to keep a long time in the sea without re-stocking of food and drinking water. This need for a technical or mandatory stoppage has brought great development to the port cities of Africa and, especially, to South Africa, the last stop in the Atlantic Ocean and the first one in the Indian Ocean.

The maritime route from Europe to Asia and/or to the West Coast of the USA via South America was so much similar to the way for Africa. All navigation in that route had to be done by skirting the tip of South America. The vessels coming from Europe to Asia sailing the East Coast of South America had to stop in cities such as Recife, Salvador, Rio de Janeiro; and Santos in Brazil, in addition to Montevideo and Buenos Aires, the last stops on the Atlantic Ocean.

After Buenos Ayres, the ships would cross the Strait of Magellan and reach the Pacific Ocean. The first port city in the Pacific Ocean was Valparaiso in Chile. From there they would go to the West coast of the USA or cross the Pacific Ocean to Asia.

The Strait of Magellan[9] is a maritime passage linking the Atlantic Ocean to the Pacific Ocean, located at the tip of the South American continent, and saving time (about two thousand kilometres) and avoiding the unruly waters of Cape Horn.

---

[9] *The Strait of Magalhães has this name in honor of the navigator Fernão de Magalhães, who crossed the channel in 1520, on his circumnavigation trip around the world by the sea.*

The South Atlantic became the most important "commercial ocean" in the world. That was the "development route". All vessel connecting Europe and Asia was obliged to follow that way.

Obviously, all kinds of investments have sprung up on both sides of the Atlantic. About that, see Annex V. The largest ship in the world in the 17th century was built in Brazil.

As can be seen on the map below, the way to Asia, along the African coast or along the South America coast, was very long routes. This was a big problem in the way of the progress of industrial revolution and must have a solution.

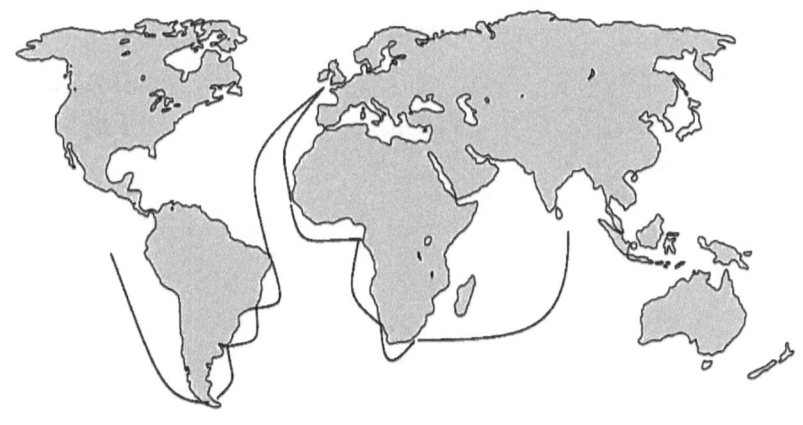

The industrial revolution in Europe, the expansion of sea routes and the increase in the consumption of raw materials were extremely beneficial for Africa, the Americas and Asia as furnishers of raw material. Africa and South America had another development factor: the scales of navigation between Europe and Asia, and between Europe and the West Coast of the United States of America.

The long period of peace in Europe, intense urbanization, technological innovations with the increase and variety of consumer goods, have substantially increased income worldwide. It was the beginning of the so called *belle époque,*[10] a period in Europe characterized by social changes, innovations in communications, the arts, transport and, above all, the peace that reigned among European countries and that fostered the development of manufacturing industry and business in general.

The introduction of the steam engine in the propulsion of the ships established more regularly times in the travels. Commercial vessels sailed at an average speed of 12 to 15 knots (something like 550 kilometres per day).

The world population grew at exponential rates, reaching over 1.6 billion inhabitants at the end of the nineteenth century, especially in North America and Oceania, which saw their populations multiplied by three, and followed closely by Latin America, which doubled its population in 50 years.

---

[10] *The Belle Époque was a period of splendor in the culture and way of life of Europe, which began in 1871 and advanced until the outbreak of the first Great War in 1914.*

World population by continent
(Millions of inhabitants)

Year	Europ Russia	North America	Latin America	Oceania	Asia	Afric	Word
1750	144	1	12	2	475	95	728
1800	192	6	19	2	597	90	906
1850	274	26	33	2	741	95	1171
1900	423	81	63	6	915	120	1608
1915	477	107	86	8	997	138	1817
1930	532	135	109	10	1072	157	2015
1950	576	167	162	13	1384	207	2509

Source: S. Kuznets. Modern Economic Growth.
Yale University Press.

However, for the African countries served by the sea routes that demanded Asia via Cape of Good Hope an unusual event occurred: the inauguration of the Suez Channel, linking the Mediterranean Sea to the Red Sea and from there to any part of Asia.

The Suez Channel were inaugurated at the end of the year 1869 and took 10 years to be built. It was 164 km long and 8 meters deep. From time to time, it receives improvements with the increase of the depth, width etc. Today it is 193 km long, 205 meters wide and 24 meters deep.

With the entry into operation of Suez Channel, the trip from Europe to Asia was shortened more than 7,000 km and ship traffic on the African coast fell drastically. The few ships that sailed on the west coast had pre-defined ports, just to take or seek some products. Thus with less traffic it began the so called "abandonment of Africa".

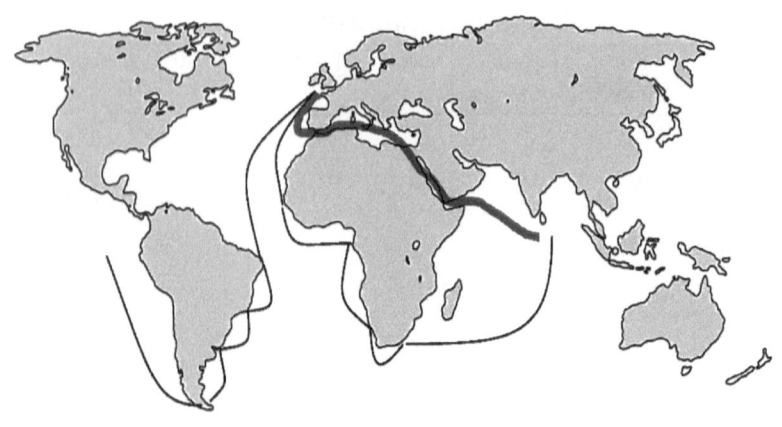

Distance from London (UK) to Mumbai (In)		
Route	Km	Navigation days*
Via African Coast	19.800	40 to 60
Via Suez Channel	11.600	Around 20

Then navigation on the African coast now relied only on the demand for its own mineral or vegetable resources.

About 20.000 ships travel through the Suez channel each year. These are ships that, if they were to navigate alongside the African coast, would be bringing progress and development. That is history. That is the past.

The success of the Suez Channel for world navigation has cherished another dream dreamed since the discovery of the Americas that is reaching the Pacific Ocean via the navigation channel in

Central America. The place chosen was Panamá, which then belonged to Colombia. The work began in 1880 under the command of France. However, the difficulties of the engineering of the time and the death of hundreds of workers, due to tropical diseases, forced the work to stop.

In 1904, a consortium led by the United States of America took over the mission to finish the job. Ten years later, they managed to connect Atlantic to Pacific Oceans. In August 1914, the Panamá Channel was open to navigation.

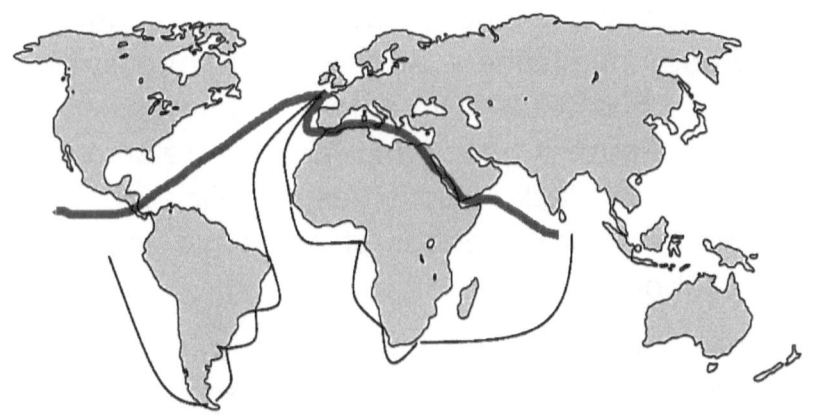

The Panama Channel reduced the distance between Europe and Asia by more than 20 thousand kilometres and introduced, along with the Suez Channel, a new and real separation between North and South beyond the imaginary Equator line.

The inauguration of the Panama Channel provoked, as had happened in Africa, a drastic reduction in the traffic of ships along the East Coast of South America. Nowadays, around 15,000 ships cross Panama Channel every year. Coast cities such as Recife, Salvador, Rio de Janeiro, Montevideo and Buenos Aires witnessed drastic reduction in ship moorings and, with that, lost gains and facility from direct connection with Europe.

As time went by, the difference between North and South became more pronounced, with the North increasingly developed and the South lost in time contrary to what was predicted two centuries ago when the presence of ships connecting Africa and South America to Europe and the USA was steadfast.

Plunged into economic decay, many countries in the South hemisphere suffered with the strong reduction of business with centres in Europe. Many countries of South America and Africa were so much affected with the lack of activities in their ports that underwent prolonged periods of economic depletion and stagnation.

This process may have caused secular development delays in many countries and territories affected by the shifts in shipping routes in South America and West Africa. Such delays would mark the future destiny of the countries below the Equator line.

To make matters worse, both continents served as a stage for the attempts of communist experiences in the twenty-century transforming Africa and South America into the hot spots of the Cold War, which aggravated underdevelopment of many areas around the South Atlantic.

We were then left to fend for ourselves. The great flow of trade development happens in the line connecting Panama to the Suez. More than 70% of business and international economic relations take place among the countries of the North and are leveraged by those two channels that were built exactly to reduce distances and save time and financial resources.

The Equator line is an imaginary line that divides the North and the South. The so called **Panamez line**[11] is a real line dividing those countries that trade manufactured goods and those countries that provide for raw material to support the manufacturing industry.

It seems that the Suez Channel and the Panama Channel have forever **symbolized the expression "third world"** and have cut off the possibility of growing economies and politically stable societies below the south of that line.

Will be true?

Are we unable to grow and take advantage of the trade with the Northern Hemisphere, and **generate business among ourselves**

Let's look at what happens today in the South Atlantic after the great historical collapse caused by the **Panamez** flow.

---

[11] *Neologism **Panamez line** is a mix of Panama and Suez*

Chapter VI
The navigation and connections in South Atlantic today

To better understanding of the navigation on South Atlantic, it is necessary to go back on the time and see what happened at the beginning of the period of the "great navigations".

In that time, the South Atlantic was the "avenue" of the great business and the way to the "other side" of the world: the Pacific Ocean.

Nature gave South America and Africa a great gift: the passage by the South Atlantic Ocean in the way to Asia. It gave also the need to take technical stops in several cities along the coasts to reach the other side of the world. This on the material plane obviously.

The passage along the South Atlantic was obligatory for long because it was simply the only way to reach Asia by sea[12].

---

[12] *History records that the Portuguese launched themselves to the sea in search of the way to the Indies.*

There is a ditto in Brazil that says: Man does; God undoes. However, in this particular case, the opposite occurred. God made the world and man changed HIS work.

To understand that history let us go to imagine two big meetings among governments, businessmen, ship-owners, bankers and other stakeholders that occurred in some time in the past. Certainly, these meetings are an exercise of imagination, but somehow they happened.

First big meeting:

Date: It probably occurred in the 1850s or 1840s or earlier until.

Theme: Construction of a navigation channel linking the Mediterranean Sea to the Red Sea and hence to the Indian Ocean.

Participants: Governments of France and Egypt, ship-owners; members of the shipping companies; bankers; businessmen etc.

Result: Ten years of work and finally the great Suez Channel was inaugurated in 1869. The United Kingdom, one of the main beneficiaries of the channel, just to part at the raise of equity capital by buying the part of Egypt's government that was bankrupted and could not repay its external debt in 1882.

Outcome 01:

Ships leaving Europe for Asia no longer had to sail all along the African coast, pass by the Cape of Good Hope, sail the east coast of Africa across the Indian Ocean to India, China and so on. The old "Silk Road" from China to Europe that had been disrupted for long time since the XIV century was reactivated by sea.

The "Suez Channel" was a tremendous success and changed forever the navigation in Africa. From then on, the European ships, going to or coming back from Asia, changed the route by the Suez channel.

Outcome 02:

The large coastal cities of Africa, which had trade with Europe as their major (or only) source of income, are hit hard and have seen reduced their main source of income and falling into secular decay.

It is good to remind that since the early 1800s the slave trade had been gradually dwindling until finally being forbidden. In 1850, the Ministry of Justice from Brazil by means of Eusébio de Queiroz Law prohibited forever the slave trade from Africa to Brazil (the big customer).

If revenues were already waning, the opening of the Suez Channel was the "bad news" for dozens of African and Brazilian cities where ships made calls to re-supply and trade.

Outcome 03:

The idea and the success of Suez Channel awakened the animal spirits of the European businessmen and investors, European governments and ship-owners made the decision to connect the Atlantic Ocean to Pacific Ocean via a channel to be built in Central America. By the way, this is the motive of the second meeting.

In fact, connecting the Atlantic Ocean to the Pacific was a dream cherished since the discovery of Americas.

Outcome 04:

The year of 1869 became a great mark for world navigation and a sad year for South America and West African, particularly for the cities located in the South Atlantic border.

Second big meeting.

Date: It probably occurred in the 1870s.

Theme: Construction of a navigation channel linking the Atlantic Ocean to Pacific Ocean Central America.

Participants: Governments of France, Colombia and USA; ship-owners, shipping companies, bankers and businessmen.

Result: Twenty or thirty years afterwards, with thousands of dead workers and the bankruptcy[13] of the first company. Finally, the construction of the Panama Channel inaugurated in 1914.

When the building of the channel began, the region where it is located belonged to Colombia. With support from the US government, the rebels of that region fought for independence and gave the USA the total right of exploitation over the channel. That agreement was renegotiated and since 1999 the Panamá Channel belongs to the government of Panamá.

Outcome 01:

The route of ships leaving the east coast to the west coast of the US or to Asia reduced in seven thousand miles. The same way, ships leaving Europe to the US and to Asia managed to reduce equivalent distance.

During the 1914 year, around one thousand ships contoured the tip of South America. Nowadays around twenty thousand ships cross the Panamá Channel.

Outcome 02:

The large coastal cities of South America that had direct trade with Europe as their major source of

---

[13] *A French company began the building of the channel in 1880, but in 1904 the USA took the building control and got conclude the channel ten years after.*

income are hit hard and have seen reduced their sources of income. The contrary happened with the coastal cities of the west side of South America. Now they were "connected to the world."

It is good to remind that two main events occurred to reduce the navigation through the South America coast since 1914. The First World War that started at the end of July, and the inauguration of the Panama Channel one month later in August 15th.

Outcome 03:

If the year of **1869** became a great year for world navigation, **1914** complete the scene with the start of operations of Panamá Channel. It was then possible to circumnavigate the world without the need to contour the tips of Africa and South America.

However, to South America and West Africa, commercially speaking, those two dates were "not dates" to be celebrated.

Well, that is history. Let us go now to seek for best days.

The commercial navigation between Europe and North America with West Africa and South America had to be re-invented. South America and West Africa had to develop their economies and trade so as compensate for the loss both had suffered with the opening of Suez and Panamá Channels.

Nevertheless, the reality of the world was much more complex. The minor conflict that began in

Bosnia with the assassination of the heir of the throne of the Austrian-Hungarian Empire extended itself to other major powers coming to involve all Europe and parts of the world, including Africa, and prolonging the First World War until 1918. In 1917, the USA had entered the conflict on side of the allies and this step was decisive to put an end to the terrible war.

The world that emerged from the war was another one. The presence and the growing influence of the USA all over the world were a inescapable reality and Panama Channel would assume a crucial function in this new international geo-economic and geopolitical scenario.

It seemed that the world could live in peace. However, at the end of the 1920s it happened the crack of New York Stock Exchange and the beginning of the so called "Great Depression" involving almost the entire world in a deep and long economic crisis. Unfortunately that world crisis helped ignite the trigger that led to Second World War that began in 1939.

What happened with South America and West Africa since then? Well with so much trouble and decay in Europe, the process of decolonization started in Africa and the efforts of import substitution industrialization were initiated in South America. However, the issue of precarious navigation between the two sides of the South Atlantic continued unresolved leading to virtual disconnection between South America and West Africa.

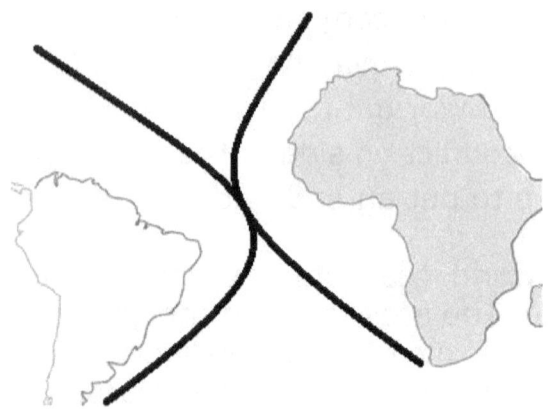

Even with industrialization in South America, especially in Argentina and Brazil, and in South Africa, the trade of manufactured goods with West Africa became too complicated. For instance, the container of both sides must go to Europe first so that to reach the other side afterwards. It seemed that Europe was located in the South Atlantic!

This crooked path doubles the freight cost, triples or quadruples the shipping time and creates every kind of imaginable difficulty.

Today a container from China to the West coast of Africa costs something like US$ 2,200. From the USA costs around US$ 1,800 and from Europe no more than US$ 1,600. However, from Brazil, Argentina or Uruguay the same container to Dakar, Bissau, Abidjan, Accra, Conakry or Lagos costs no less than US$ 3,000.

If businessmen of South America and West Africa intend to trade between themselves the chances of success in the transaction are jeopardized because of the high cost of maritime freight as well as the lack of regular transport lines between both sides.

The loss in trade transaction is not just the loss for exporter or importer by the payment of double the freight value, the loss is also due to the fact that there are no shipping companies in the SARIS region. Companies have to hire two services: one service is the rent of containers and the other is the transport of the container. Therefore, the company loses competitiveness and the country loses scarce foreign currency.

Chapter VII

A new deal for the South Atlantic

*The Regional Integration System of South Atlantic – **SARIS***

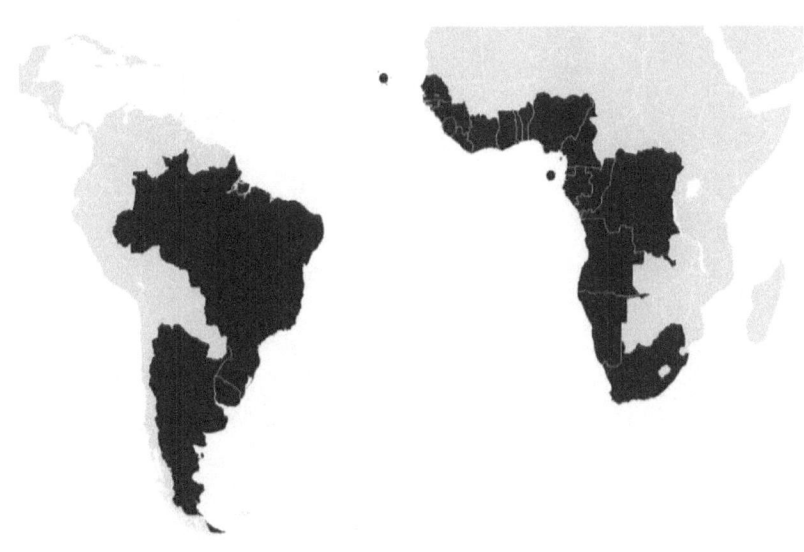

The SARIS is the natural market of South America and Africa.

When we talk about the "nonexistence" of direct maritime lines linking South America and Africa or that our merchandise must go to Europe firstly before arriving in final destination, everybody asks why this "illogical" way prevails in the logistic arrangement.

Obviously, there is one or another transport line between South America and West Africa, but what exists is very much less than what was necessary to meet the pent-up demand of two continental blocks as those existent in West Africa and South America.

The ship owners say that there is no volume of merchandise to be transported between the two blocks. Of course, it is right that there is no cargo volume to ten ships per week between South America and West Africa. However, there is cargo for one or two ships. Certainly there is.

I would say that one or two ships per week leaving the coast of South America and making one, two or three stops in different regions in Africa is sufficient to begin. So, the increase in exports and imports between both sides would be enough to pay for freight, rent of containers and insurance by "outside companies" of the SARIS.

What can we do to make it happen?

There are three options.

The first one is to let all things as they are just now and to continue with loss of markets on both sides of South Atlantic. Lost opportunities to increase the bilateral trade and reliance on clients of the North hemisphere. Such an option is not the ideal solution because we Africans and South Americans would be always under the dependence of big international companies of navigation for all business decisions we need to take.

The second option is developing deals with the navigation companies to establish some routes linking the east coast of South America to the West Coast of Africa in its route to Europe.

This can be made according to the maps below by using the existing routes with some little arrangements. Today the merchandise is loaded in South America ports, travels to some European port for transshipment and the goes on to the final destination.

Some merchandise for Africa to South America follows the same way. The stop and transshipment in Europe is required. This "crooked" path disrupts business, doubles or triples the time between leaving and arriving in destination. This more than doubles the value of freight and creates every kind of difficulty imaginable.

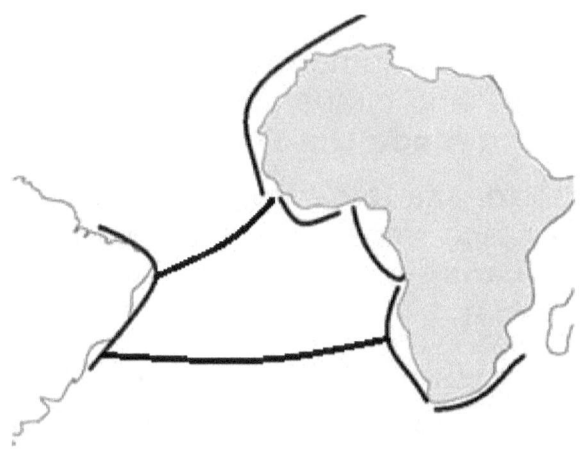

The third option (a bold option that depends on the independence and free will of each government of the countries bordering the South Atlantic), it is the way to achieve the social and economic development of the countries among the bordering of South Atlantic.

As mentioned in the above chapters, there are virtually no direct lines among the countries of South America and the West African countries. This fact, for itself, prevents the formation of strong business among our countries and businesses. In addition to preventing the creation of strong economic ties, the lack of direct shipping lines creates all kinds of impediments for the very existence of trade among our peoples.

Certainly, you have heard dozens of times that "union makes the force". That is true. The union of peoples or countries makes a group stronger. Suez and Panama Channels are the proof of that.

A shorter maritime route to the Indian Ocean was needed and imperative. **The Europeans gathered and made the Suez Canal.**

A shorter sea route from Atlantic to the Pacific was needed and imperative. **The Europeans and the Americans got together and made the Panama Canal.**

Now, Just now, the maritime connection between West Africa and South America are imperative and needed. Here begins the **third big meeting** that can change the course of navigation in the South Atlantic and, of course, change the course of the development of both sides.

The **first big meeting** created the Suez Channel.

The **second big meeting** created the Panama Channel.

And just now is coming the time to the **third big meeting**. The meeting to approach neighboring countries of the South Atlantic looking for a feasible and sustained solution to the shortfall in maritime connection to facilitate the trade among our countries.

The Third big meeting

Date: Someday in the future. I hope a close future.

Theme: Constitution of a navigation system to link the west coast of Africa to east coast of South America.

Participants: All neighbouring governments of South Atlantic; ship-owners; members of the shipping companies; bankers; businesspeople and representatives of a great economic superpower.

China can be the biggest guest invited for this meeting. Why not? The Chinese can become the big partner of this new deal for South Atlantic, once the creation of a shipping company to operate in South Atlantic **could be part of the great Chinese Belt and Road Initiative (BRI).**

It is widely known that China is becoming the powerhouse of the world because of its sustained high growth performance in the last 30 years. As China is now the second largest economy and the biggest exporter country. It is natural and legitimate its intention to assume an increasing role in the world economic affairs. The times of low profile of China in the geo-economic diplomacy are gone.

That is why the Chinese President, Xi Jinping, announced what is now known as the "Belt and Road Initiative (BRI), formerly "the One Belt, One Road" (OBOR). Launched in 2013, with the stated purpose of promoting the economic prosperity of the countries along the Belt and the Road and regional economic cooperation, thereby strengthening exchanges and mutual learning between different civilizations, and promoting world peace and development.

According to Bessa Maia (2019), the BRI consists of both 'One Belt' and 'One Road'. The 'One Belt' component refers to the Silk Road Economic Belt, which extends from China to Southeast Asia, South Asia, Central Asia, the Middle East and Russia, and further to Europe. The Belt is 'land-based' and comprises highways and railroads which connect China with numerous countries in Asia and Europe. The Belt is expected to grow into six economic corridors, which span China and many parts of Eurasia.[14]

In its turn, Bessa Maia asserts that the 'One Road' refers to the Twenty-First Century "Maritime Silk Road", consisting of sea roads which connect the significant ports in China, other parts of Asia, Africa, and Europe via the South China Sea, the South Pacific Ocean, the South Indian Ocean, the Red Sea and the Mediterranean Sea.

China has been more active economically and diplomatically across Africa and South America, particularly since 2005. China's increasing presence in both regions has been reinforced under President Xi Jinping and likely to continue to expand under the development of the BRI.

As China has already extended its BRI, especially its "Maritime Silk Road" component to

---

[14] *Cf. Bessa Maia, José Nelson. "The Belt and Road Initiative in Latin-America: a single opportunity for China" in: The New Silk Road and the Portuguese Speaking Countries in the New World Context. Edited by Fernanda Ilhéu, Francisco Leandro and Paulo Duarte. Lisboa: Instituto Internacional Macau, Amigos da Nova Rota da Seda, 2019.*

Africa and South America, the Chinese could assume a driving role in the maritime connection between West Africa and South America. The engagement of China in this initiative would be not only important in geopolitical terms because China would perform a protagonist role in the South Atlantic but also contribute to expand trade and speed up economic development in the countries of Mercosur and those of the West Africa coast. And a bridge linking East and West of South Atlantic is all we need to develop a big relationship between these two continental blocks that look to each other through the seas.

Results awaited: A fast, cheap and trustful service of transport among the hub ports of the region on both sides of the South Atlantic.

Outcome: Increase trade links among the several countries in the SARIS region and creating conditions to lead development to all countries bordering the South Atlantic.

In fact, we are watching nowadays a mass migration from Africa to Europe and other parts of the world. We are also watching the poor countries of South America and Africa struggling to escape underdevelopment. But most of those countries are governed by backward political systems that close and otherwise hamper connection with the globalized world. Thus, changing the navigation on South Atlantic would be crucial to the development of both continents and to overcome the political stalemate that has kept so many countries behind.

Conclusions

When we check what happened with Africa and South America, after the advent of Suez and Panama Channels respectively, we could ask:

- Oh my Lord, why did you abandon South America and Africa?

Certainly, God would answer us.

- I did not abandon neither one nor the other. When I created the Atlantic Ocean, it was not to separate the two continents. Instead, it was precisely to unite them. The Atlantic is the route. Someone else already said: sailing through distant seas is necessary.

Then? What are we going to do?

If we, neighbors and joint owners on both sides of the Atlantic, and free and independent countries that we are, do not have the capacity and competence to take care of our destiny and our business, we can be sure that someone will do this service in our place, as it has been done for a long time.

There are no shipping companies, either African or Latin American, doing freight transport between West Africa and South America.

And when someone does the service that we could or should do, certainly the decisions of what to do, how to do and who to do will not be ours, but of the "owner" of the business.

In the same way, if there is someone doing this freight transport between West Africa and South America, it is because this business is profitable. Everybody knows that there is no free lunch. In addition, if it is profitable, who gets the profits from the business? Certainly not us, the neighbors on both sides of South Atlantic.

There is a need for a reunion, a great meeting among the neighbors of the South Atlantic in the search for a solution to the void that exists in navigation in South Atlantic.

Even an island, it is not an "island". No country is required to be alone or isolated. The idea to approach South America and Africa is a global proposal, which "aims" to explore the huge business opportunities existent on both side of the Atlantic Ocean.

International flows of goods and services point to Africa as the great emerging market. A more detailed analysis of global geopolitics had pointed to the South Atlantic as the region of greatest potential for the development of international business. South America has great potential and Africa is, probably, the richest continent of the world in natural resources.

There is a significant flow of ships along the East Coast of South America and along the West Coast of Africa, but these two flows do not communicate. On the contrary, they are isolated.

Then we could ask: Who will gain with the transport and with the exploitation of the potential of South America and Africa? if we let the "things" how they are, certainly our participation in the profitable deals of the SARIS will be minimum. It all depends on us, bordering countries of the South Atlantic.

As it was said at the beginning of this book, the Atlantic Ocean can be a meek and calm creek or a brave and troubled sea. Everything depends on the intention of the governors that border it. It is necessary to develop connection routes between these two maritime flows or create conditions to new companies to explore these unexplored routes.

If we, South Americans and West Africans, do not take the lead in these negotiations, soon it will be completely reliant on external companies to make some business with the North countries or among ourselves.

Annex

Annex I
Lloyds – The biggest navigation company in South Hemisphere.

The shipping company *Loide Brasileiro* was founded in February 1890, during the administration of president Marshal Hermes da Fonseca. The English word "Lloyd" was translated to "Loide" in Portuguese.

The late nineteenth and early twentieth century were the golden period of world shipping and *Loide Brasileiro Company* soon became the largest company in Brazil, becoming the biggest company below the Equator line.

At the beginning of the World War II in 1939 the company had 122 ships that gave Brazil leadership in the maritime sector throughout the South American continent. Loide lost some ships during War, sunk by German submarines, but even so continued to expand in both cabotage[15] and long-haul shipping.

By this time, the name of the company, Loide in Portuguese, returned to its original English form

---

[15] *Cabotage is the navigation service practiced from port to port, within a country or region. This name comes from Sebastião Caboto, a 16th-century Venetian navigator who mapped the entire East Coast of the United States and Canada.*

Lloyd. Lloyd's national and international tariffs and rates were extremely high thanks to its monopoly in the Brazilian market.

While shipping companies around the world were looking for efficiency, Lloyd maintained its high tariffs, anchoring itself in the Brazilian shipping monopoly. However, with the opening of Brazilian transport shipping to foreign companies, competition among ship-owners for greater shares in the import and export market had intensified. The fierce competition, overstaffing, mismanagement, high costs and debt overhang drove Lloyd to the brink.

In the early 1990s, Lloyd's ships began to be arrested by international courts. Labor debts associated with pre-existing debts defined Lloyd's bankruptcy and the company was extinguished at the dawn of its one hundred years, mired in debt until the last hatch.

Annex II
The Thailand channel

Singapore has earned its place in the business world through its port, which is one of the fastest and safest in the world.

Singapore and its port are located at the tip of Malaysia and it is a port of concentration of goods (Hub Port) for the whole region of Southeast Asia.

All ships from Southeast Asia to the west, or from the west to Southeast Asia, must pass through Singapore and the Malaka Strait. It seems perfect: A hub port in a place of obligatory passage.

With the exploration of its port Singapore has developed and is today one of the most prosperous countries in the world.

However, what seemed perfect, it is under a threat. The government of China and Thailand are advancing studies for the construction of a channel in the Isthmus Kra, in the territory of Thailand.

With the construction of this channel, ships now passing through Singapore will have a highly feasible alternative, reducing by more than a thousand kilometers on their route that represents two days of navigation.

Of course, this channel will not completely affect Singapore's trade. The business structure developed so far in Singapore is quite solid, with a banking and financial system, agile and with strong connections around the world.

However, in the competitive world we live in, two days of sailing can make a big difference in the great Southeast Asian market.

Who lives will see!

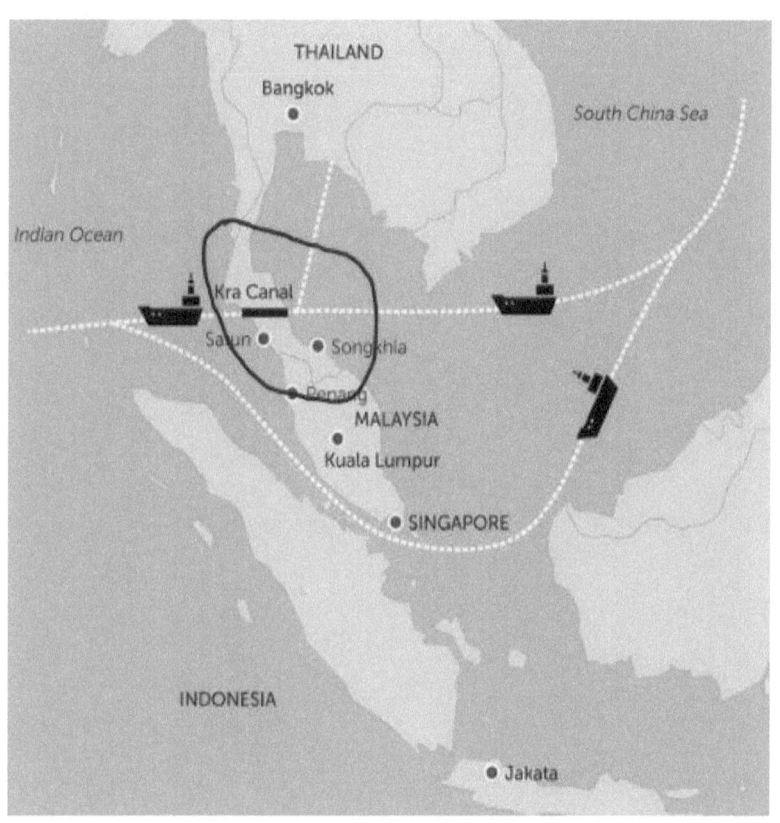

Annex III

The movement of containers in African countries.

Manufactured goods are, normally, transported in containers. The movement of containers in the ports gives a good idea of the vitality of a country's foreign trade.

The table following shows the movement of these containers in the main African ports and in South America. The total handling of the container includes the loading and unloading of full or empty containers.

The vast majority of containers are made up of 20 and 40 feet containers. To account for the number of containers handled, the TEU (Twenty (feet) or Equivalent Unit), is used, that is: all containers are "transformed" into 20-foot containers. Roughly speaking, the 40-feet container counts for two containers.

We also put the same table, container handling in China, the United States of America, Singapore, Hong Kong, and Brazil.

China, with more than two hundred million units (TEU) in 2018 is by far the largest container handler in the world.

The United States and Singapore, two other giants in container handling occupy second and third places, with forty-three million units and thirty-two million units, respectively.

In Africa, except Egypt, South Africa, Kenia, and Morocco, all other countries move less than one million containers per year.

Ghana, Ivory Coast, Angola, and Senegal, are the highlights in Sub-Saharan Africa, with more than 500,000 containers per year.

Ghana, close to one million containers per year, presents a consistent and stable growth. This growth is not isolated; there are other countries in the same way. Benin, Cameroun, Gabon, Republic of Congo, etc., have presented firm growing also.

In South America (Mercosur block), Brazil is the biggest handler of containers, with a little more than 10 million units, followed by Argentina with 1,7 million of TEUS, and Uruguay, close to one million.

Container traffic by country Thousands of TEU´s				
	2016	2017	2018	
World	695.000,0	710.000,0	752.000,0	+
Africa				
Angola	913,0	1.000,0	706,0	-
Benin	348,0	349,0	387,0	+
Cameroun	340,0	342,0	353,0	+
Djibouti	910,0	987,0	987,0	+
Egypt	7.186,0	7.377,0	7.430,0	+
Gabon	518,0	519,0	550,0	+
Ghana	900,0	900,0	921,0	+
I. Coast	625,0	705,0	663,0	-
Kenia	1.076,0	1080,0	1.200,0	+
Morocco	3.965,0	3.979,0	4.570,0	+
Mozambique	449,0	450,0	432,0	-
Namibia	255,0	260,0	265,0	+
Rep. Congo	355,0	355,0	386,0	+
S. Africa	4.662,0	4.454,0	4.634,0	+
Senegal	530,0	540,0	497,0	-
Sudan	538,0	540,0	551,0	+
South America - Mercosur				
Argentina	1720,0	1.741,0	1.750,0	+
Brazil	10.300,0	9.925,0	10.049	+
Uruguay	811,0	888,0	887,0	-
Others				
China	195.276,0	199.551,0	213.719,0	+
Europe	87.446,0	90.867,0	96.135,0	+
USA	49.527,0	50.181,0	51.425,0	+
Singapore	31.710,0	32.668,0	33.600,0	+

Source: World Bank

Annex IV

The economic blocks in Africa and South America

To better research data from the economic blocs in South America and Africa, access the site address of each one:

ECOWAS

https://www.ecowas.int/

CEMAC/UDEAC

http://www.cemac.int

SADC

www.sadc.int

MERCOSUR

https://www.mercosur.int/

Annex V
The biggest vessel of XVII century

To support the commerce with Asia, the companies had to do local investment in both sides of South Atlantic, to get sweet water, food, and services to repair the vessels, after long times in the sea. These investments promoted a huge development in Africa and South America port cities.

On the Europe-Asia route, going or coming, vessels had to do several scales in South Atlantic, in the Africa side or South America side.

These scales was obligatory. The vessels had not autonomy to keep a long time in the sea without re-stocking of food and drinking water.

This need for a technical or mandatory stoppage has brought great development to the port cities located on Africa and South America.

To support the scale of the vessels, the companies had to do local investment to get sweet water, food, and services to repair the vessels, after long times in the sea.

In Brazil, especially in Salvador, Rio de Janeiro, and Recife, the industry of repair and construction of vessels grown enough. In Rio de Janeiro it was constituted a shipyard named Galeão, in 1659, to repair and mainly to construct vessels using the resistant and softwood of the tropical forests.

Under orders of _Sá e Benevides_, Governor of Rio de Janeiro, they began an ambitious project: The building of a galleon, a big commercial vessel that received the name of _Padre Eterno_.

The _Padre Eterno_ (_Eternal Father_) was a vessel classified as Galleon, built-in from 1659 / 1663, to transport sugar to the Companhia Geral de Comercio do Brasil, CGC (General Company of Trade of Brazil).

Later, when CGC come to broke, the vessel were sold to the Portuguese Crown and became part of the Portuguese navy.

According to *Mercurio Portuguez*, a periodical published in Lisbon in XVII century, the *Padre Eterno* was considered the biggest ship of its time.

The beginning of the construction of Padre Eterno was in 1659, and it was launched in the sea in December of 1663. The maiden voyage happened in 1665, to Lisbon.

The characteristics of that "giant of the seas" are impressing for that time. It had 53 meters of length and had capacity to transport two thousand metric tons of goods and 300 mariners.

However, the *Padre Eterno* was not just a transport ship of goods. It was also a battleship with 144 artillery pieces.

At the end of the seventeenth century, the Eternal Father sank into the Indian Ocean.

The sinking of the Eternal Father is a mysterious fact that does not know the causes until today.

In October of 1665, that Periodical published the following news:

"*On 20th of this month of October, began to enter in the Lisbon Port, the fleet from Brazil with forty vessels. In the fleet came the famous Galeon Padre Eterno, the biggest vessel that there is in the seas*".

Engraving of vessel *Eternal Father* (**Padre Eterno**) at the entrance of the Tagus River (Rio Tejo), in Lisbon, Portugal. This engraving is in the book ***Description de l'Univers***, from 1683.

References:

- ALVES, Jorge Luís dos Santos Alves. "As Relações Brasil-África Subsaariana no Contexto da Atividade de Inteligência". *Revista Brasileira de Inteligência*. Brasília: ABIN, nº. 13, 2018.

- ARBACHE, Jorge; MAIA, José Nelson Bessa (2019). *O Futuro da China e as oportunidades para o Brasil*. Rio de Janeiro: Conselho empresarial Brasil China (CEBC), Setembro, 2019.

- BIRD – IPEA (2011). *Ponte sobre o Atlântico Brasil e África Subsaariana - Parceria Sul-Sul para o desenvolvimento*: Brasília: Banco Mundial e Instituto de Pesquisa Econômica Aplicada, 2011.

- CARVALHO, Josiane Rocha; NUNES, Raul Cavedon (2014). "A ZOPACAS no contexto da geopolítica do Atlântico Sul: história e desafios atuais". Revista Perspectivas, Vol. 7, n. 13, 2014.

- MAIA, Altair (2016). *Logística Internacional – O desafio do Atlântico Sul.* Brasília: Editora Kiron, 2016.

- PEREIRA, Ana lúcia Danilevicz; PORTELA BARBOSA, Luísa Calvete (2012). *O Atlântico Sul no contexto das relações Brasil-África*. São Paulo: *Século XXI*. vol. 3, nº. 1, 2012.

- SARAIVA, José Flávio Sombra (2012). *África Parceira do Brasil Atlântico: Relações Internacionais do Brasil e da África no início do século XXI*. Belo Horizonte: Editora Fino Traço, 2012.

- VIEGAS FILHO, José (2016). *A Segurança do Atlântico Sul e as Relações com a África*. Brasília: FUNAG, 2016.

- PENHA, Eli Alves (2017). *A Segurança e a Defesa do Atlântico Sul no Âmbito da Cooperação Brasil-África: Vontade e Capacidade de Soberania*. Rio de Janeiro: Instituto de Geografia/Universidade do Estado do Rio de Janeiro – UERJ – apresentação em PowerPoint disponível em:

< defesa.gov.br/arquivos/ensino_e_pesquisa/defesa_academia/cedn/XIII_cedn/a_seguranca_e_a_defesa_do_atlantico_sul_no_ambito_da_cooperacao_brasil-africa.pdf>, 2017.

Site adresses:

ECOWAS

https://www.ecowas.int/

CEMAC/UDEAC

http://www.cemac.int

SADC

www.sadc.int

MERCOSUR

https://www.mercosur.int/

The Observatory of Economic Complexity - www.oec.com

World Trade Organization – WTO
www.wto.com

The Author

Altair de Sousa Maia is an economist graduated at the University of Brasilia (UnB) with specialization in International Trade.

- For a full decade, he worked in the Ministry of Foreign Relations and the former Ministry of Industry and Commerce (MDIC) in Brasilia/DF.

- He has lectured as a professor in the Catholic University of Brasilia and at the school of Finance Administration (ESAF) at the Ministry of the Finance.

- As a professional he has consulted on various widely diverse projects all connected with import-export. He has participated in trade fairs and missions in many countries throughout Africa, Europe and the Americas.

Today he is a consultant in international affairs specialized in African matters. Speaks on these matters throughout Brazil and abroad.

E-mail to contact: altair2001@yahoo.com

Other books of the Author

World World, Vast world

Our carelessness with nature is endangering human life on Planet Earth. The advent of plastic has contaminated soils and seas, forming huge dumps, both on land and at sea. Desertification is another great challenge for humanity, and Africa's great green wall is the most eye-catching work in an attempt to stop the force of the Sahara Desert.

Africa: A business from China.

This is an analytic book researching the Chinese presence in Africa. What will happen with Africa in one or two hundred years?

International Logistics.

Trade between Brazil and Africa is almost nonexistent. At most, it reaches 3% (three percent) of the total traded by the African continent. This is largely explained by the lack of maritime transport between these two continental blocks. Brazilian goods destined for Africa firstly go to Europe and just then to their destinations.

The Commercial Relations Brazil Africa.

Work developed in partnership with José Flávio Sombra Saraiva. José Nelson Bessa Maia and Gustavo Pontes Maia, analyzing the issues related to the Brazil x Africa trade and outlying a proposal for overcoming the logistics bottleneck.

Griots - Sounds and Colors of Africa

Relating diverse aspects and moments of the African life and the new era that begins with the Chinese presence in the entire continent.

Tribute to Jonathan Makeba

A deep analysis of the obstacles to African development, especially in the Sahel region. Exciting story unfolding on the Burkina Faso border with Niger, involving politicians and executives in a multi-million dollar investment.

Baobab - Scenes and facts of Africa

A collection of texts narrating facts and scenes from the daily life of several African countries on trips made over more than ten years throughout the African continent.

Guide of export for micro and small companies.

As its name implies, it is a work designed to "open" the doors of International Trade for Micro and Small Enterprises and to acquaint entrepreneurs with the terms and practices of international trade.

The mutilated rose.

Female excision practiced throughout the African Sahel and some countries in the Middle East, where more than 3 million girls are mutilated each year. It is a high-risk operation by the form and conditions as it is practiced.

Masks and Skulls

An interesting story about the search for sacred objects for the initiation ritual in Candomblé/Vodun in the region between Benin and Nigeria, in Yoruba´s land. That is the region from where, in the past, most of Brazil's slaves came.

The dino who burned his foot

A children's book that children recommend for adults. A step back in time when the Dinos dominated life on earth.

Children of the Moon

A relentless hunt for albino blacks to turn their parts into lucky charms.

Mucubal - A different people.

Customs of an African tribe that gapes at us but has a certain "sense of reality".

Trip to Bissau

Guinea-Bissau is one of the poorest countries in the world. A million and a half people in a small country on the West Coast of Africa. However, it is a country with high agricultural potential and a coastline considered the most fishily of all of Africa. In this small country the political dispute is fierce and, occasionally, tragic.

Brasil e Guine – Laços Indissoluveis

Brazil and Guinea - Indissoluble Ties

An analysis of the socio-cultural-commercial relations between Brazil and Guinea Bissau